A LITTLE
LESS OF A
Hot Mess

to: Katie

Here's to
being a little
less & a hot
mess!
xoxo
Clayssaur

A LITTLE LESS OF A HOT MESS

The Modern Mom's Guide
to Growth & Evolution

KAITLIN SOULÉ, LMFT

THE
collective
BOOK STUDIO

Library of Congress Cataloging-in-Publication Data available.
ISBN: 978-1-951412-41-8
Ebook ISBN: 978-1-951412-66-1
LCCN: 2021911087

Manufactured in China.

Printed using Forest Stewardship Council certified stock from sustainably managed forests.

Cover design by Andrea Kelly.
Interior design by AJ Hansen.
Typesetting by Maureen Forys, Happenstance Type-O-Rama.

10 9 8 7 6 5 4 3 2 1

The Collective Book Studio®
Oakland, California
www.thecollectivebook.studio

Dedication

This book is dedicated to my three beautiful children, Mia, Alex, and Jack . . . you are everything beautiful about this world. May you carry home with you in your heart, always remember who you are, and live your life in a way that feels authentic and free to you. Tony, the love of my life, thank you for being exactly who you are, and for loving me for exactly who I am. Mom and Dad, thank you, endlessly, for giving me both roots and wings, unconditional love, and for encouraging me to dream big. To the women brave enough to go on a growth journey, even when it feels impossible to find the time or space, remember that you were born beautiful and holding everything you need to be brilliantly you.

Table of

Contents

REWRITE

YOUR

STORY

Chapter 1

YOU'RE INVITED TO EVOLVE

"Tell me, what will you do with this one wild and precious life?"

—MARY OLIVER

I am writing this book from a place of my own (imperfect) evolution. I picked one of my favorite quotes, by Mary Oliver, because it says so much in so few words—the idea that the opportunity to live a big, full, wild, and precious life is there for the taking . . . but only if we're willing to grab it. I am writing this book as I am actively learning to listen to my own intuition, to stay still enough to hear my own voice, and to challenge the ways of thinking and being that hold me back from living in alignment with my values. I am writing this book because I believe women want a more intuitive way to evolve and grow, and ultimately feel more "at home" in their own skin and with their REAL selves. All too often, women are made to feel like we have to be "perfect" at parenting, in our careers, and in our relationships in order to be worthy . . . I'm here to call bullshit on that nonsense. I believe that if we aren't living imperfectly, we aren't truly living at all.

Listen, I'm no stranger to the life of a hot mess mom; sometimes I think I might have written the book on it. Through lots of trial and error, and some futile attempts to be something other than who I am, I have learned that I can still be a great mom, therapist, change-maker, wife, friend, and human AND not have all my shit together. I've also learned that I can be a little less of a hot mess by doing my own personal growth work—by slowing down and turning inward (instead of outward), practicing sitting with life's massive uncertainty, taking smaller steps toward bigger change, and choosing to lead with my core values.

As a therapist who specializes in helping women do the work of healing and change, and as a mother who is navigating life with three young children, I know how uncertain, challenging, beautiful, and chaotic life can feel. I've lived the crazy, I've heard (all) the crazy, and I know that at the end of the day we're all really just on a quest to find a piece of ground we can stand on that feels like our own, that feels both peaceful and joyful . . . and I believe it's our right to find that space. The belief that we need to be "broken" in order to seek help when it comes to our mental or emotional health keeps SO many of us from doing the work of getting unstuck and living well . . . this "sick" model of mental health is stale and in need of reform. You aren't broken if you're wanting a better way forward—instead, you're paying attention . . . you're alive! We owe it to ourselves to commit to evolving, not because we are "sick," but because we all get stuck sometimes, and we want to get "unstuck" and find a better way forward.

THE THREE *R*s OF MODERN GROWTH AND EVOLUTION

From where I sit, growth, evolution, therapeutic work (whatever we choose to call it) is a process of rewriting, restoring, and reclaiming. When we look at our past, where we've been and what we learned about ourselves, we are able to revise and "rewrite" a better way forward. When we restore our relationship with the woman in the mirror (who we are now), we reconnect with our purpose and get clear on our values and the kind of life we want to live! When we do the work of rewriting and restoring, we are freer to take imperfect action and reclaim our voice, our purpose, and take up MORE meaningful space in the world! Personal growth is about staying curious: taking a wide-lens view of ourselves and our life with an open mind, and then identifying some things that aren't working for us anymore so that we can make the changes we need to make in order to move through the world freely and wholeheartedly.

I'm going to hit you with a truth bomb here—we don't just owe it to ourselves to grow and evolve, but we owe it to our children, too. As the famous psychologist Carl Jung said, "The greatest burden a child must bear is the unlived life of its parents." As women, we are often made to feel guilty for our own evolution, as though it's one big inconvenience for everyone around us. But let's consider this: if we don't show our children that their growth doesn't have to stop after they stop physically growing, who will? Let's also consider this: if we don't allow ourselves to evolve, and we stay stuck in negativity, darkness, or sameness out of fear . . . then what price will our children pay? Let's start this book journey together with the acknowledgment that we don't want our children to suffer due to our unwillingness to look at our own, for lack of better word, shit! This book is intended to invite you into the process of getting unstuck in the places you need to SO that you can grow and evolve, both because you deserve to live a big, full, awesome life AND because your children need to see you doing that in order for them to have permission to do the same.

OK, cool, let's proceed.

WHAT IS (IMPERFECT) GROWTH AND EVOLUTION?

On the quest to find or redefine ourselves, we often get lost or feel stuck. We are inundated with tips and tools when it comes to our physical and emotional health, but hear this—if those messages are making you feel worse, you aren't alone. Here's why: while probably delivered with good intention, there are some *real* issues when it comes to the messages put out there in today's version of the personal development space; they are often empty and rigid. Apparently, I just cut right to the chase there. But seriously . . . I don't want to be sold another product or clean eating challenge that will take away all my problems and, if I'm lucky, a few pounds too. Why? Because I'm going to drop the ball. I'm not going to stick with it and then I'm going to slip into all kinds of self-loathing and feelings of not being enough.

I am not saying every piece of advice on social media is "bad"; in fact, I've learned a lot in that space, and I think if used mindfully (which is freaking hard sometimes) there is some good stuff there. I am saying that we don't need any more for-profit businesses trying to tell us what's going to make us feel good and whole and then have us feel like we're failing when we don't live up to the rigid expectations put forth by, I'm going to go out on a limb here, a white male at the top of a pyramid scheme. And what does it mean to "just be positive," or "cut out the people in my life who don't understand me"? Let's pull back the reins a bit. It all just seems a little extreme and, yes, unrealistic. The truth is, we don't need to be told how to be the best version of ourselves; we need to grant ourselves the permission to open our minds and hearts to the opportunity to imperfectly evolve. In order to truly evolve, we need to be willing to get uncomfortable and unlearn some things that have gotten in our way.

There has been some incredible research and writing on imperfect evolution, even though they might not call it that.

Brené Brown, one of my own personal guideposts for evolution, describes wholehearted living best in her book, *The Gifts of Imperfection,* by saying: "Wholehearted living is about engaging with our lives from a place of worthiness. It means cultivating the courage, compassion and connection to wake up in the morning and think, 'No matter what gets done and how much is left undone, I am enough.' It's going to bed at night thinking, 'Yes, I am imperfect and vulnerable and sometimes afraid, but that doesn't change the truth that I am also brave and worthy of love and belonging.'" We were born with permission to be fully human, in all of its pain and glory; however, somewhere along the way we lose sight of that truth and start to believe that we are only worthy if we are smart enough, pretty enough, small enough, privileged enough (insert anything else self-defeating here).

MY INVITATION IN . . .

Writing has been a way back, forward, and home for me. This book and these sentiments have been on my heart for a long time. As a therapist, I'm in the midst of a career that is literally built on helping people do the work of imperfect evolution, and yet I too doubt whether or not I am qualified to be sitting here writing this very book you are reading. Like so many of us, I am really skilled at getting in my own way with stuck beliefs and old stories. I'm sure you have plenty of your own, but here's what is in my fun bag of unhelpful beliefs: "Who am I to write a book? There are people way more qualified!" "I'm too ordinary," "I don't have the time to write a book . . . I'll never finish," "It's SELFISH for me to take more time away from my kids for me to write this." Yes, those are some of the shitty things I tell myself that have historically kept me feeling shame or anxiety and keep me playing small. If you share some of the doubts listed above, I am not surprised . . . as women we are especially conditioned to stop ourselves before we start and tell ourselves we just simply aren't enough or worthy.

If you're lucky, when you're a kid you get encouraged to reach for the stars, try new things and continue to grow . . . but then suddenly when you become a mom the message seems to change. When we're not doing our growth work, the message we hear is "I actually need to stop growing and evolving so that I can be what everybody else needs me to be . . . there's just not enough room for my needs and theirs." That message shatters and shrinks our sense of self beyond caretaker, and then we feel like we're failing at a way of life we never fully choose. Caretaking, nurturing, managing, planning . . . it's all part of being a mom, and it can be overwhelming and all-consuming (especially in the baby phase), but when we get so lost in that role, we abandon all the other parts of ourselves that make us a whole person. Look, we didn't suddenly lose our own needs, wants, and desires when we had children; it's just that getting our needs met and going toward our goals and desires became a hell of a lot more complicated. So I am coming up alongside you in this book (think of me like your new BFF who happens to be a therapist) so that we can work together to change our narrative around what it means to be a mom these days . . . we deserve to grow, change, and evolve along with our children.

Here's a little bit about the start of my motherhood journey: becoming a mom shook me to the core, in all kinds of ways, and for the first time in my life I was filled with a sense of purpose I had never known before and a deep desire to give my children all the love and tools they would need to survive this messy world. But do you know what else came with that sense of purpose and desire? A big dose of fear and doubt. It took me a while to get out of the postpartum haze (I had three babies in less than five years) of survival to recognize that I could benefit from my own therapy work. So I checked out the view from the other side of the virtual therapy room and started the "work." It was a collection of moments and experiences that invited me into the hard and messy task of peeling back the layers, challenging the old stories, healing past wounds, integrating, and getting back in touch with my authentic self. Hear this: I am still on the journey (and will always be) of rewriting my story, restoring my most whole and authentic self, and reclaiming my voice and way forward in this wild world!

In doing my work, personally and professionally, I am realizing that there has always been so much more to me than I allowed to show up in every room. I recognize that throughout the years, and for all kinds of reasons (all of which we'll talk about in this book), I had fallen into the habit of making myself "smaller" to try to squeeze into places I didn't fit, so that I could make OTHER people more comfortable, all the while feeling out of alignment with my own values. I am realizing that as I'm growing and evolving as a human, mother, therapist, and writer, the only person I need to make sure I don't let down is ME. If I am lifted, they are lifted (my husband, my kids, my clients). Period. End of story. OK fine, clearly it's not the end yet, so stick with me here.

Years before I became a therapist, I cast myself in the position to be the one who others came to for advice. I was often described as "grounded" or the "rock," and I offered up my heart and mind freely to help others figure out their next move or navigate their path. I now realize that helping and guiding is a gift, and deeply a part of me, but not at the expense of my own well-being. We can sink ourselves trying to keep others afloat. Also, let's be honest, it's often easier to focus on other people's problems than it is to look at your own. That truth stings a bit, right? But I know you can either relate to this and/or think of somebody in your life who seems to always have the answers for everyone else as a way to deflect from their own discomfort.

Now that I've learned that the invitation to healing and change is ALSO mine for the taking, instead of posing the question of "Who am I to write this book?" I pose the question, "Who am I NOT to write this book?"

A SNAPSHOT OF MY IMPERFECT EVOLUTION . . . WHAT DOES IT LOOK LIKE?

Picture this: It's 5:45 A.M., and I'm feeling proud of myself for FINALLY doing what I planned and getting up before the kids. Side note: I find that I start my day so much better when I have a few minutes to have a cup of coffee while it's quiet, get a few minutes of meditation in, and then dive into writing. Also, when it comes to writing this book, there is literally no other time in my life to write except for the wee morning hours . . . by the time it's night I feel I've had every ounce of creativity sucked out of me and I'm done. I suppose I could tell you all the reasons it can feel so hard to get up before the kids, but it probably goes without saying that the number one reason is simply: I'm tired! I know I don't have to tell you this, but the days are long, the bedtime routine is exhausting, and at the end of the day all I want is an hour or two to myself to get stuff done. "Get stuff done" is really code for staying up too late watching Netflix, without the "chill" part, because I will likely fall asleep on the couch ten minutes in. OK, back to my story. It's 6 A.M. and I've just finished my meditation, I've got my hot cup of coffee right next to me, and I open my laptop to start writing . . . it's all good and blissful until said coffee spills all over the couch. Clearly it was an oversight on my part to put the coffee on a soft surface like a couch, but oversights are kind of my thing. UGH. But the next part is the part I think is most worth sharing . . . I didn't freak the F out. Why? Because like I said before, oversights and mistakes are something I've had a lot of practice at. Truly, I am a perpetual klutz, always have been, I'm often late, and always forgetting things . . . some might call me a "hot mess." I am good at cleaning up messes and moving on. So that's what I did. I sprayed the toxic chemicals on the already pee- and food-stained couch, wiped it up, and kept on writing. Yes, this is my life, and probably like yours it's full of missteps and things that didn't go to according to my plan. Here we are, though; in spite of all of the things that go "wrong," big and small, we keep showing up to our life.

Imperfectly evolving is about continuing to show up for yourself, your family, and the stuff that matters the most to you EVEN when it's messy. It's not just about being a "badass" or "boss babe," because while those words make for cute hashtags, I'm not sure how we define those things, and they don't seem to leave room for the real parts of life, the ones where you feel like you're not nailing it. In a world where not much is certain, error, mistakes, setbacks, or whatever we decide to call them, are certain. Imperfectly evolving is about being on your own side, holding the *both and* of life, and deciding that you are your own wisest teacher and dearest friend. It's a journey that I'm choosing to take, and you can take with me, where we give ourselves permission to walk forward and back home to our most authentic and integrated selves so we can live messy, big, joyful lives.

YOUR INVITATION IN . . .

My voice is mine, my story is mine, and I have a lot to say. So this is me coming up alongside you, not above you, to share what I'm learning as a practicing human, therapist, mother, and wife about the process of growing into the person you were born to be. This book is an invitation to better understand yourself, to accept and (even) celebrate the messiness of life, so that you can move, unapologetically, toward your most meaningful life. In this book, through my own stories, insights, and discoveries I invite you into the process of evolving and learning to live (imperfectly) well.

The twelve invitations that I share with you in this book are yours for the taking—and I see them as a path toward getting unstuck, living well and wholeheartedly and as . . . a little less of a hot mess. And by the way, just by virtue of you being curious enough to pick up this book and read it, you are already starting down the path of imperfect evolution. So before we walk further down that path together, let's talk about what imperfect evolution means and some of the roadblocks that tend to get in our way.

THE THINGS THAT GET IN OUR WAY . . .

There are a lot of things that can get in our way when it comes to accepting life's invitations to continue to evolve, but for the sake of simplifying things it seems the roadblocks are best categorized as the ones we create for ourselves and the ones the world creates for us.

To put it simply, there has been a long history of stigmatizing getting help for issues related to mental health both due to a lack of cultural emotional intelligence (more on that in a minute) and to old worn-out beliefs about therapy being only for the "sick" or "severely mentally ill."

In his book *Working with Emotional Intelligence*, Daniel Goleman discusses research done by the Harvard Business School that decided that emotional intelligence is a much higher predictor of success (in fact double) than IQ and tech skills combined. Thankfully, there is increasingly more work being done on the topic of emotional intelligence, and I think that is changing the trajectory of the way we feel, as a society, about the importance of mental and emotional health. Still, at the most basic level, most of us would likely agree that we weren't exactly encouraged to talk about our emotions or distressing feelings as a child. The overt messages may have sounded like "stop crying . . . crying doesn't solve anything," "I'll give you something to cry about," or "big girls don't cry." The more covert messages may have looked like being dismissed when expressing big feelings, or you may have received attention only when you were feeling positive emotion and left to fend for yourself when dealing with sadness, anger, or anxiety. When you are little and you're abandoned with messy or difficult feelings, the message is clear: it's not safe or OK to feel. So what did we learn as a result? We learned that it's easier (and safer) to just shut it off, or to speak up and show up only when we're "good." We are humans living in a complex world, and I don't care what the Instagram self-help gurus say, it's unrealistic to think we will spend most of our time in positive emotion. So when we're taught to not show up for life unless we're expressing unicorn and rainbows vibes, we are put in the position to cut off parts of ourselves and our experience. And that, my friends, is the place in which things like anxiety, depression, addiction, and low self-worth are watered and grown.

If you happen to come from a family who celebrated going to therapy or addressing mental health struggles, I want to give your family a big old socially distanced/virtual hug (thanks to COVID), but for so many that wasn't the case. This dynamic is most obvious to me when I am doing an intake interview with a new client or family that I am starting to see in my practice and we come across the question of whether or not their family has a history of mental health disorders. Every once in a while, people can give me a definitive "yes," but that's usually because somebody in their family is very obviously mentally ill and their illness has caused a lot of disruption. But most of the time, people's answers go something like this: "Now that I think of it, I think my dad may have a struggled with a lot of anxiety because he didn't leave the house often, and drank a lot." If you have a member or multiple members of your family who used drugs, alcohol, or even food in ways that were excessive—they were likely using those negative coping mechanisms as ways to numb out or avoid their anxious, sad, or lonely feelings, because they never learned a better way. And you certainly aren't alone in that family dynamic; the hard and, sometimes ugly, truth is that is most of our stories. If we aren't allowed to face our fears or our human emotions, or we don't know how to, we are often forced to find unhealthy ways to numb or avoid. Emotions are an essential part of the human experience (without them, we wouldn't be human) and they're a strong force of energy that moves through us—they need somewhere to go. If we don't give our emotions a way to rise and fall, build and release . . . they will find a way, and as I'm sure you've experienced,

Personal growth is about staying curious: taking a wide-lens view of ourselves and our life with an open mind, and then shifting or changing the things that no longer serve us well.

they don't always pick the path of least resistance (sobbing to a stranger in the grocery store, having a panic attack in your kid's school parking lot, or treating the people you love the most like a piece of old trash . . . I've been there too). Let's just not blame this all on our family of origin; let's also talk about the education system (or lack thereof) around mental and emotional health that existed when our grandparents and parents were young. I do notice that the younger clients I see in my practice tend to be much more well versed in emotional vocabulary, which gives me hope that things are improving when it comes to social and emotional learning. I have friends and colleagues who work as therapists in the school systems and they put their heart and soul into advocating for more resources for the schools they work in, but the truth is there often simply isn't a big enough budget allocated to mental and emotional health. Often there is just ONE therapist, and maybe one intern, for an entire school district. Personally, I think having mandated classes on mental health throughout our children's education would be so much more effective than spending a whole class learning how to put a condom on a hypothetical penis (I mean, a quick YouTube tutorial would do), or fear-mongering teenagers about STDs and the risk of getting pregnant. Side note: Sex education is really important, but we can do so much better there if we focus on both its beauty and its risk/potential outcomes. What if we focused as much on mental health as we did on outdated history lessons (remember the study I talked about earlier done by HARVARD that found that EQ was more important than IQ)? Point and case.

So how do we bridge the gap? The bottom line is help and education for our mental and emotional health SHOULD be for everyone and start young. There is a lot of reform that needs to be done in order for mental health to be more widely accessible, and (spoiler alert) I don't have the answers here in this book. We have a long history, as a society, of minimizing and utilizing comparative suffering when it comes to a lot of things, but especially mental health. We've all likely said some version of this, "Yes, COVID sucks and it's hard on the family, but at least we have our health and each other." OK, so that's some good use of finding perspective, but just because you haven't lost a loved one or the ability to put food on the table for your family doesn't make the struggle any less real, painful, or impactful. Or maybe you struggle with mild anxiety or depression . . . and that "mild" struggle isn't less of a struggle for you by virtue of the truth that there are people who have it much worse than you do. To stretch this point further, the fact that there are people living on the streets, hearing voices and isolated from their families, won't make your experience of anxiety or depression any less shitty. It's a little bit like saying that only people with serious diseases should have access to health care. What we miss when we assume that mental health is only for the "truly sick" (a term I strongly dislike) is both the power of preventive care and the fact that we leave out over half of the population that doesn't qualify for a severe mental health diagnosis. Do you need to have diabetes to eat more greens and move your body? Nope, we sort of just know that's what we need to do to be healthy. Of course, whether we choose to do that or not is up to us. But when it comes to our mental health we often don't even know where to start, or how to start, so we wait for the other shoe to drop, or for a crisis to happen before we reach out for help . . . and we can do so much better than that.

One of my favorite quotes, from none other than the queen Maya Angelou: "When we know better, we do better." And when it comes to parents, I believe it's a global truth that most of us want to do the best we can for our children. I believe that parents can both love their children deeply AND be really inept at guiding them through their emotional experiences. So while we likely agree that some big systems need to change in order for access to mental health education and help to improve, it's also true that it starts right here with us moms.

I suppose there are quite a few roadblocks we come across on our path to healing and growth, but the one I see most often is fear. Simply fear. When I started off as an associate, I was incredibly lucky to work under two highly skilled therapists and clinical directors. Jennifer Shannon, anxiety expert and book author, was one of those women, and I'll never forget the theory she holds around what is beneath every type of anxiety/worry/fear/stuck point. Jennifer said, in some version, that while people come into therapy with many different presenting problems, they are likely afraid of one of these two things: 1. Getting kicked out of the tribe (so to speak) or 2. Dying. It took me a while to understand what she really meant by that, but after sitting with thousands of clients who come to me (mostly) for help with anxiety . . . I have to say, she nailed it. People need to feel that they belong, somewhere and anywhere. People also need to survive, yet with each day that passes they are moving one step closer to dying (I know, depressing but true). Here's where I would like to add a layer to my wise colleague's theory—in order to belong and stay alive we feel a deep need to avoid disruption by keeping things the same even when we know, deep down, they could benefit from changing. In the psychology world, we refer to this very human behavior as keeping homeostasis. It's true that when we choose to keep homeostasis, we don't risk the uncertainty of what will happen when we disrupt the waters. It's also true that when we choose to avoid disrupted waters, we don't ever get to make it out of the harbor. And from what I know about myself, and most people I come across, we want to get out of the damn harbor . . . we're just afraid of what we might have to face in the big open ocean.

LET'S WORK TOWARD CHANGE . . .

Please allow me to go all therapist on you for a minute. I want you to close your eyes, right here and right now, and imagine you're sitting in a shady harbor, with calm waters and familiar scenery. It's predictable there, and you're very familiar with the scenery around you. Imagine that far beyond the opening of the harbor, and past the walls, you see a glimpse of the most blue/green water you've ever seen and a beautiful island in the distance. You wonder what it would feel like to bask in the sunshine, and even more, you wonder what's on that island waiting for you. Do you choose to stay in the harbor or check out what's beyond it? Do you stay stuck, and maybe even cozy, or do you detach from the buoy, get a bit uncomfortable, and explore what life is like when you're willing to open your eyes and see what evolves?

A NOTE BEFORE WE GO FORWARD . . .

In my clinical work, and in my own life, I've recognized that there are certain places we tend to get "stuck" as women, and the invitations in this book offer us movement forward . . .

a chance to get unstuck. My hope is that this book will help you build, or strengthen, a healthy foundation, a knowing really, from which you can be free to evolve and step into your most powerful, authentic, and whole adult self. Each invitation into growth acts as scaffold for the one that follows—so it will be most helpful to read the book in the order it's written. In order to deepen the understanding of the concepts talked about in this book, I've shared stories from my own (very imperfect) evolution as well as stories from the many clients I've had the gift of working with in my clinical practice. Please note that the actual names of my clients and identifying details have been changed in order to maintain anonymity. My hope is that you'll find yourself in these stories and that you'll see a hopeful way forward on the path to becoming a little less of a hot mess, and a lot more of the imperfectly evolving/badass mama living her life expansively and joyfully! So please trust yourself and this process of (imperfect) evolution EVEN when it feels strange! Keep your open mind (and I'll try not to go too woo-woo on you) and a journal and pen close by so you can do some reflection work at the end of each invitation/chapter.

Throughout this book, you can follow the journal prompts to move through and expand upon the concepts we've explored. The prompts are short and sweet and intended to help you move from knowledge to action. Remember, when it comes to learning new mental and emotional health skills, just like everything else in life, you might find it difficult, and you might even suck at it at first—so give yourself some grace. I leave you with this: when your toddler was learning to walk for the first time, and she fell down, did you say, "Ugh! You're never going to get this . . . you're the worst!" I know it's kind of laughable, because of course you didn't say that . . . you told her to keep on trying and that she was doing great, you may have even told her you were proud of her—what would it be like if you started doing that for yourself?

Take a moment to reflect on why it is you bought this book in the first place (beyond the really fun cover). Taking it a bit deeper, what do you think is holding you back from living more freely, fully, and imperfectly? And then what do you hope to get from reading this book? If this book does what I hope it will, and helps you down your path of growth and evolution, what would your life look like? What kinds of things would you do for pleasure, what would your days look like, what would you have more of, what would you have less of? I promise this will be the most open-ended question . . . there is no "right" answer, just be boldly imperfect and go for it!

The Practice

Chapter 2

YOU'RE INVITED TO REFLECT

"For it's our grief that gives us our gratitude,
shows us how to find hope, if we ever lose it.
So ensure that this ache wasn't endured in vain:
Do not ignore the pain. Give it purpose. Use it."
—AMANDA GORMAN

So who the heck were you before they called you mom? It's a simple question with a pretty complicated answer. For me, it's sometimes hard to remember who I was before I became a mom . . . because so much has happened since then. When we become "mom" our hearts, responsibilities, and mental and emotional loads expand SO greatly that it can be hard to remember what we did yesterday, let alone who we were just five or ten years ago.

But at the very start of this journey together, I am going to challenge you to dive into the question of who you were before. Because if we don't look behind us (even when it's uncomfortable or downright painful to do) we might miss the pieces of the puzzle that help us understand who we are now, what we have right here in front of us, and what direction we want to be heading in. I can't tell you how many times I've heard some version of this in the therapy room: "You aren't going to ask me about my childhood, are you?" or "This is the part where we blame everything on my mom, right?" or "I've been in therapy before, and all we talked about was my past and it wasn't really helpful." I get it . . . all of those sentiments. It is true that solely focusing on our past, or why we are the way we are, won't help us solve the here-and-now struggles we face and/or move forward. But it is ALSO true that we need to be willing to look at where we've been in order to understand what has helped us develop the stories we tell ourselves, how we created the beliefs we hold, and why we have developed the positive and negative coping mechanisms we use—to put it more simply, why are we the way we are and why do we move through the world in the way we do?

The work of growth and evolution starts with being willing to take a look at where we've been, determine what we TRULY care about right now (what we cared about in our twenties is likely very different than it is now), and then make the changes we need to make so that our time and energy are being poured into the things that we most value. Before I go hating on the haters—I recognize that fear and misunderstanding have a big role to play in this schema. So many people are afraid to take a deeper look at their own lives out of fear of what it will unleash or uncover, and they sure as shit don't want to risk you doing the same because they fear they'll get left behind in the dust as you evolve. Remember, we aren't doing this work for the haters—we are doing this work for ourselves, for our children, and for our own unique big "why?!"

MY INVITATION IN . . .

So I'll start the very overwhelming task of trying to summarize some of the most impactful moments of the last thirty-seven years of life like this: I am Kaitlin . . . well, at least most of the time. Sometimes I go by Katie. When I was a child it was mostly "Katie," and it wasn't until later, somewhere between college and the "real world," that I decided I wanted to go by Kaitlin. I never felt sure about it, and I still don't. Some days I feel more Katie than Kaitlin, and some days I feel more Kaitlin than Katie. I don't know why that is; I feel insecure about this sometimes, because I feel like I SHOULD prefer one name over the other (or just pick), but I go back and forth around which one feels more like "me."

I grew up on a winding road with lots of room to roam and play, and I was blessed (and still am) with two incredible parents who encouraged me to dream big, try new things, and prioritize education. I am the youngest of three. I have two brothers and most of our childhood days were spent using our imagination to create worlds that didn't exist in the pastures and creeks. We'd spend all day "digging to China." Why there? Who knows. My first love was figure skating. I'll never forget the way it felt to glide across the ice, or the way the blades sounded cutting through it. I quit figure skating in eighth grade because I came to the hard realization, with the help of my dad, that I was giving up way too much of my time and freedom to be a "so-so" figure skater who was on a fast track to developing the "wrong" body type (or at least that's what I was made to believe). There are few things more awkward than having your first period arrive during a competition weekend where you had to squeeze yourself into a skintight costume, especially before you knew about tampons. I didn't feel proud that I was becoming a woman; I felt betrayed and even angry at my own body.

Letting go of figure skating would be the first truly "hard" choice I ever had to make. Maybe even before figure skating, my first true love affair was music. My father would play the guitar for us most nights and sing everything from the Beatles to Johnny Cash. I remember, even as a young girl (maybe eight or so), my eyes welling up with tears when he would play one of my two favorite songs: "Sad Little Girl" or "Leaving on a Jet Plane." I know, you're probably thinking that's pretty sadistic and a bit strange for an eight-year-old to love such depressing songs . . . but I did. I hung on every word and felt all the feelings, almost forgetting that the song was a story separate from my life, instead it was as though I was them, and they were me. I was an empath (for better and worse) from the start. As a young child, and still today, music was the pathway into my emotions, allowing me the private space I needed to learn to feel and deal. Here's the thing though (as any "good" empath knows), you don't want to inconvience others with your big emotions or feelings. So when the music moved me to tears, I did my best to make sure nobody else noticed. I can see now that music was my first invitation into being curious and moved by what other people decided to make of their own life's story.

So I decided when I grew up I would, without a doubt, either be a songwriter or a screenwriter. In high school I got decent grades, played sports, and had a solid group of friends, some of whom are still in my life. My maternal grandma passed away when I was seventeen years old, and it was my first experience with grief and loss. You know those moments in time that never leave you? Well, finding out the news of my grandma passing, while standing in the hotel lobby with my mother in the college town I was about to move to, was one of those moments. We had made the trip all the way to Colorado solo, and were excited, almost even gleeful, at the prospect of getting a taste of the opportunities ahead. I'll never forget the sound of my dad's voice when he called my cell phone that day and said, "Can I talk to Mom?" In his voice was the knowing that he was about to break our hearts with the news. Another image forever etched in my mind is my mom slowly and calmly walking herself over to the lobby couch, having just received the news, so she could sit down and let out a quiet sob. Just the night before we were all eating Chinese food together, grandma was drinking her bourbon and soda water, laughing, and we were listening to my oldest brother play the guitar. My mother and I held hands and sat in silence for most of the flight home. I remember feeling confused around whether I was most sad that my grandma passed or that my mom had lost her mother . . . now I know it was both. It wasn't until that moment in time that I realized how finite and fragile life is, and that it can go from joyful to gut-wrenching in the matter of seconds.

When I started applying to college, I thought becoming a creative writer felt too far-fetched, or not concrete enough. I decided I would study journalism, and I would become a writer of other people's stories, a truth teller. Then the path got a bit twisty, in some really good and hard ways (as it does), and I decided to take my first internship at a local news station in San Francisco. From there, more opportunity arose—including one of a lifetime, where I got to go to Italy to work as a production assistant at the Winter Olympics. I lived it up . . . as one does at age twenty-two living in a once quaint (until we arrived) village in Italy in a five-star hotel. That internship led me down a career path in TV, where I moved to LA and would go on to work around some really powerful and (some) shady people in the entertainment industry . . . including Donald Trump on the show *The Apprentice*. I mean, I could probably write an entire book about what it was like to work in such close proximity to the Donald (I was the production assistant to his daughter Ivanka), but for now I'll leave that one up to your imagination. But before I move on, can I just say . . . he presented

EXACTLY as sexist, narcissistic, and problematic then as he did as our president.

A lot happened in LA—I worked for some of the richest people on earth, got paid pennies, hustled to work in an industry that seemed hell-bent on using people (TV), and fell in what I thought was "real" love for the first time. Sure, I had been in relationships before (ish), but this time it felt different. I reconnected with my second-grade crush on MySpace (yes, remember that?) and in all that loneliness and searching for myself, I was intent on making a relationship that was unhealthy and out of balance—I gave too much of myself to somebody who was in a lot of turmoil and pain, and broke my own heart when it didn't work. This is probably where I should mention that I had a real strong propensity to try and "fix" other people without yet understanding that people don't change unless they're ready or willing to. I could have saved myself a lot of pain if I understood that earlier . . . but isn't that just the way life works, hindsight is always twenty-twenty. "I reached out so far, but I couldn't find your hand." Those were the words that I wrote down in the midst of my post-breakup depression. That breakup led me through the doors of a therapy room for the first time ever. Do you know that statistically most people only go to one session of therapy and don't return? Well I, the future therapist, became a part of that statistic. I thought I just needed a space to cry and share my feelings with somebody who wouldn't judge me, or tell me something along the lines of "told you so." I needed a container for my sense of loss and pain . . . and that it was, for one session. Who knows why I didn't go back . . . maybe I got exactly what I needed, or maybe I just told myself I did. Later, I would find my way back into therapy and realize I needed and deserved so much more than just that one session—not because I was broken and needed to be fixed, but because I was (am) worthy of healing, and I needed to learn to stop listening to the noise, and learn to listen to my own inner wisdom.

After all that searching for myself in a la-la land (which was fun but not my place in the world) I was homesick, not for the home I grew up in, but for San Francisco—a place that felt familiar, a place that I felt had opportunity without façade. So I packed it all up and moved to "the city," where I decided I would take some time to figure out what was next for me . . . because reality TV wasn't it! I realized that while I loved story, those weren't the stories I wanted to tell. Then it was random jobs in advertising (not a good fit), a few new boyfriend situations (also not great fits), lots of barhopping, apartment rentals, and trying to find my place in the world often in very counterintuitive and messy ways.

Enter Tony. My husband, and the man I get to call my children's dad. I won't bore you with all the details, but I'll just say this . . . after all the BULLSHIT you deal with in your twenties as a young woman, he was a breath of fresh air. It was easy, he was (and still is) my soul mate, my rock, my best friend, and my reason for wanting more. For the first time ever, I didn't take on the role of the "fixer" in the relationship, because he wasn't broken. I didn't hide the parts of myself that I felt ashamed of, because he celebrated them. From the moment I met him, I felt whole—not because I needed him to "complete" me, but because he held up a mirror, reminding me of my wholeness. He loved me as I was—which, of course, felt both vulnerable, foreign, and so good. Perfect? No, not by a long shot, but he and I had (and have) what it takes to stand the test of life's ups and downs, twists and turns, and all the stuff in between. As a firefighter

As we move through this journey of imperfect evolution, we must start with our own story and a willingness to look back so that we can better move forward.

who loved his job, Tony inspired me to get into a helping career, and so I figured maybe I could finally learn how to use my "fixing" skills on people who actually wanted to be fixed. And then shortly into my career I would learn, in some challenging ways, that therapy is about so much more than "fixing." I would learn that even people who feel broken are already whole, and that while we can equip people with the knowledge, skills, and tools they need to change or heal—it (still) has to include a willingness to take a look at the parts of ourselves and our lives that we often feel too ashamed or scared to look at.

I completed my graduate program in 2013, got married two months later, started working on the ungodly number of hours needed to get licensed (3,000), and had two babies in fifteen and a half months . . . I mean no big deal, right? I got licensed in 2015, started my private practice, and had our third, and last, baby two years later.

Now here I am, in this life with three kids, an imperfect and beautiful marriage, with a full practice, and still the sense that there is always something bigger ahead. I started writing this book in the middle of a global pandemic because I was bored trying to homeschool three kids and manage a full work schedule . . . just kidding, in all honesty, the pandemic gave me the kick in the ass I needed to stop waiting for the perfect time to say the things that were in my heart to say. So while I'm leaning into my creativity more than ever these days, and that feels good, I find myself needing a lot of reminders (some from myself and some from the universe) to slow the hell down and just be content where I am. You see, I have a propensity to "do" my way out of my feelings (we'll talk about that lovely maladaptive coping mechanism in the feelings chapter) but I am learning to pause, take stock, and just "be" in the messy middle of life these days.

This, of course, isn't all of my story, but it's the highlight reel and CliffsNotes version. I have to be honest in saying there are some painful parts that I have left out, because I too am imperfectly evolving, and doing my own healing work. I hope this will remind you that, when it comes to your own story, it's important to be tender with yourself and to meet yourself where you're at. Vulnerability is incredibly powerful, and all the rage these days . . . however, we don't need to be vulnerable at the cost of our well-being and mental health. In other words, we don't actually have to be an "open book" and share all the tender parts of ourselves on Instagram in order to have a stake in the vulnerability game. Sometimes, when we tell our story too soon, too fast, or to the wrong person—it isn't held as tenderly as it needs to be and we can feel flooded, overwhelmed, and worse off than we were before. When it comes to vulnerability, what's most important is that we're willing to be honest with *ourselves* about all the parts of our experience . . . and if we have a few people in our life who have earned our trust enough to get to know our "truth," well, that's a beautiful and powerful thing.

So what does my story have to do with yours anyway? Well, this is the part where I can help you learn to unpack your story and the way it has informed your beliefs by unpacking my own. When I took a deeper look at my own story, I can see where I formed some beliefs that might have served to protect me when I was younger (or at least I thought they did at the time) that no longer serve me as a grown, healthy adult. Let me connect the dots from one part of my story to a limiting or negative belief (I'll use those terms interchangeably) that I have had to learn to change in service of my own growth and health.

Remember the period story? Well, when I got my period for my first time, it wasn't that I didn't know it would come or what it was. It was just that it was treated as "gross," or an inconvenience—something not to be talked about, or bothered with, and something that would hinder me from doing the things I enjoyed comfortably, like sports. Especially since I went to a Catholic school where celebrating a woman's body wasn't a top priority (or a priority at all), it also wasn't talked about as a positive part of female development in health class. So there I was, at eleven years old, stuffing my curvy and muscular body into a skintight costume with light beige tights, feeling disgusting and praying that no blood would come through and out the fact that I was (heaven forbid) becoming a woman. In my mom's defense, she didn't know I was feeling this way, and if she did I believe she would have supported me, but I didn't speak of it. I just kept it all inside and kept on skating. Like so many young girls do, I choose to stay stuck in my own feelings of shame so I wouldn't risk making other people uncomfortable or feeling hurt by my experience. The negative belief that I started to formulate as a result of the period incident, and would later reinforce time and again, was two-part: "Your body is not something to be celebrated, and instead of tuning in to uncomfortable physical sensations, tune out and avoid." While it made sense to hold that belief at the age of eleven, given the experience I had, it didn't serve me to bring that belief into being a teenager or an adult. Because I'm at therapist, I've gotten pretty good at drawing the line that connects my beliefs and my behaviors, and I attribute my unhelpful beliefs about my body to many instances of

betraying my own body, not listening to its cues, and CER-
TAINLY not honoring or celebrating it. But you know what
was most powerful in shifting my (shitty) beliefs about my
own body? Becoming a mother. Giving birth to three babies,
and enduring a few miscarriages, showed me what my body
was capable of . . . the amazing things it could do, and how
it could heal.

Looking back and putting my own life story on a time
line (i.e., what impactful events happened at what age), and
then identifying what belief I formed from that event, has
been the place from which I invite myself to grow. If we
want to grow, we don't just stop at identifying the unhelpful,
hurtful, or total bullshit belief that we formed along the way
and then sit in them . . . no, we do the work of unlearning it
and relearning beliefs, or taking perspectives, that are more
true and more helpful. I am still in the process of unlearning
the beliefs and behaviors that keep me stuck and healing the
past wounds that hold me back from living as all of me . . .
and I think it's a forever journey.

YOUR INVITATION IN . . .

Sometimes it's hard to know the exact impact that a limiting
or old belief has had on you or your life, and that's okay. It's
not important that you connect all the dots or find a "reason" for all of the missteps, wrong turns, and past hurts. At
the end of this chapter, you'll find a prompt to help you do
the work of mapping out the most impactful pieces of your
story so that you can better understand how and why you
handle things the way you do, and give yourself the invitation to change that patterned response. But first, without
using a ton of outdated psychobabble (lingo created by the
white male founders of most psychological theories), let's

dive a bit deeper into what limiting beliefs are and how they impact us. Limiting beliefs, sometimes called negative beliefs or the stories we tell ourselves, are created by the automatic and uncensored thoughts and feelings that we experience.

At the very basis of CBT (Cognitive Behavioral Therapy) is the idea that our thoughts, feelings, and behaviors are all connected. It goes like this: something happens, we get triggered, we have some kind of automatic thought about the triggering event, and then we have feelings about it (including physical sensations), and then we act in a way that lines up with the way we feel.

Let's use an example of a client I once worked with, to help us better understand the concept of how limiting or old beliefs can keep us stuck. Janet was a client who came for help with her social anxiety and her struggle to have what she called "healthy" relationships. She told me a story of a recent incident on a girls' night that made her feel incredible embarrassment and even shame. Janet, after a glass of wine or two, told a group of fairly new mom friends that she had been abused as a child. She made a fairly flippant comment about her abuse, and when the women didn't respond she felt her skin flush, and the panic set in. The intensity of her feelings of shame got worse the next day, when she sent out a "thanks for having me" text and got no response. Here is how her trigger, thought, feeling, action chain went: Thought: "I said too much, they think I'm a freak." Feelings: anxiety, panic, embarrassment, and shame and increased heart rate. Action: avoid the women at school pickup so she didn't have to deal with further feelings of shame or embarrassment. The thing about Janet was, she had a lifetime of experiences of feeling unheard or like it wasn't safe to tell her truth, so while the women probably were just busy and didn't mean harm (which later we found out to be true), she was going down the rabbit hole of shouldn't-haves and shame. This experience reinforced her limiting and old belief that it's safer to keep your feelings to yourself and to trust nobody. It's no wonder that with a belief like that Janet had a hard time allowing herself to be seen enough in order for others to fully connect with her . . . which, of course, made her feel more alone, moving her further away from the possibility of having healthy relationships. Over time, we worked to create a better understanding of how this old belief led to her acting in ways that weren't helpful and ultimately to create a new belief and new behaviors that could help her move in the direction she wanted to go—really the direction we all want to go, more REAL connection.

LET'S WORK TOWARD CHANGE . . .

The point is, no part of our story happens in isolation from the other parts and without impact . . . so if we can better understand our story and how it has informed our identity (which is really just made up of the beliefs we hold and the actions we take), we can also change them in service to our own growth.

It becomes clear, then, that as we move through this journey of imperfect evolution we must start with our own story and a willingness to look back so that we can better move forward. I see this as a three-step process. Step 1: Dive into your own story so you can understand where and how you formed your life's narrative. Step 2: Decide whether those thoughts and beliefs that make up your story lead you closer to where you want to go, or farther away from it. In other words, do those thoughts/beliefs that fuel your behavior serve you anymore? If you can't find that even just one or two beliefs don't serve you anymore . . . congratulations, you aren't even human. All kidding aside, we all have ways of moving through the world that no longer serve us, and it may take you a while to figure out what those things are—that's normal, give yourself lots of grace. Step 3: Once you've identified some of the limiting thoughts and beliefs that you are ready to say "byeee, it's been real" to, you're ready to start the work of transforming them into more powerful beliefs—ones that allow you to change your story, and your life!

Think back on your life and try to identify some of the moments, experiences, or events that were most impactful . . . what beliefs might you have formed because of them? Ps: This can be a lot to think about, so consider breaking it down into a time line (i.e., from birth to age five, from age five to ten, from ten to fifteen, from fifteen to twenty, from twenty to twenty-five, from twenty-five to thirty, and so on).

Identify one of those beliefs that still serves you well and you want to hold on to.

Which of those beliefs seem to no longer serve you or keep you stuck?

What do you think would change for you if you were able to let go of or transform those unhelpful beliefs? What would your life look like without those limiting beliefs that hold you back?

Knowing what you know now, is that belief totally true? Whether or not it's true, is it helpful . . . does it serve you in the "right now" moment as a grown-ass healthy adult? If not, what belief might be more helpful in moving you toward your values?

Pick one of the limiting beliefs you identified above (one that was formed because of a life event or a series of life events) and answer these questions: Who taught you to believe that, or what life events taught you to believe it? How old do you feel when you say that belief out loud? Now create a belief that is MORE helpful and MORE true. After you create your new belief, decide how you will live into it.

Pick ONE practical thing you can do within the next twenty-four hours to live this belief, i.e., make a phone call, start a project, go for a walk. I encourage this to be a small action!

If you are able to live into this new belief more often, what would change in your life six months or a year from now?

Chapter 3

YOU'RE
INVITED
TO FEEL

"I am here to keep becoming truer, more beautiful versions of myself again and again forever.
To be alive is to be in a perpetual state of revolution. Whether I like it or not, pain is the fuel of revolution. Everything I need to become the woman I'm meant to be next is inside my feelings of now. Life is alchemy, and emotions are the fire that turns me to gold. I will continue to become only if I resist extinguishing myself a million times a day. If I can sit in the fire of my own feelings, I will keep becoming."

—GLENNON DOYLE, UNTAMED

WHY I'M INVITING YOU . . .

What Glennon said . . . but seriously, could it be said any better? To be alive is to feel . . . once we stop feeling, we stop really living. It seems crazy to think that we actually have to be reminded to feel our feelings, but the truth is, while we are born knowing exactly how to feel, somewhere along the way we learn (and relearn) that feelings are dangerous, and that having the very things that make us alive makes us weak. Think back for a hot second to when your baby was born. He/she/they came out of that womb screaming, red-faced, with fists up—as if to say "I am HERE, I made it . . . see me, hold me, love me." We saw them, we held them, we loved them. When we were little ones, before the world laid all of its "stuff" on us, we knew how to show our feelings only in ways that reflected our exact emotions. When we were excited, we jumped up and down and twirled around. When we were sad, we cried our eyes out. When we were angry, we stomped our feet and let our voices be heard. When we felt loved, we gave big wet sloppy kisses and tight hugs. Children let us know exactly how they feel, and while it can be difficult for us to manage as adults (OK fine, downright maddening sometimes), it is pure, simple, true, and just as it should be.

But then, life happens; it throws both its beautiful and relentless layers at us. Somewhere along the way, and for all kinds of different reasons, we distance ourselves from our feelings out of fear that feeling them is not acceptable, dangerous, or both. The irony is, and as you'll see through the stories that I share in this chapter, it's quite the opposite—the MORE we turn away from, instead of toward, our feelings, the more we abandon ourselves and diminish our ability to navigate complex human experiences such as loving and losing. And you've likely discovered this already, but no amount of avoidance of feeling will make hard things less likely to happen . . . in fact, it will only make them more challenging to cope with when they do (inevitably) occur. We either feel now or pay later.

MY INVITATION IN . . .

I wish it were the case that simply by virtue of being a therapist I was somehow immune to emotional struggle—but that's just not the case. I am learning to accept that having the knowledge and putting the knowledge into practice are two very different things. I imagine I am probably better off than the average Jane (sorry, Jane) when it comes to feeling my feelings, but as you'll hear in this story, I am far from immune to struggling with my own desire to avoid my emotions when they're . . . well, hard to sit with.

A couple of years ago, I decided to attend my first-ever therapeutic retreat with other mental health professionals. While I attend conferences, talks, and professional development experiences, taking a full weekend for my own therapeutic benefit was something that "other" people did . . . until I became one of "those" people. Even though the weekend was being led by a therapist (my own) I deeply trusted, I couldn't help wondering what in the hell I was getting myself into. Would we sing kumbaya, hold hands, sit around a candlelit circle? I had no idea, but I got on the plane anyway and prayed that there would be some free time built into our schedule . . . and wine. I had to push through so many of my own narratives (which I'll dive into more in Chapter 4) in order to convince myself to spend the money and show up for myself, and it was worth every penny—that weekend spent on the beautiful coast of Southern California with a group of incredible women was one of the greatest gifts I gave my adult self.

But if I'm being honest (which I'm committed to being with you), what happened between getting off the plane and arriving at the retreat is important to share. There was some lag time between landing in Orange County and when I was due to arrive at my destination, and lag time and I don't go so well together. I felt this familiar and incessant need to fill the spaces in time by "doing" instead of just allowing myself to arrive. My life back home, three kids and a full-time job deep, was feeling a bit exhausting and too predictable . . . so I deserved a little self-care time, right? This is where I call bullshit on my own self. Listen, I am a huge advocate for us women to take the time we need to pour into ourselves, but on that particular day my choice to buzz around and fit as much into the very little time I had was about so much more than that. I couldn't see it right away (we often don't when it comes to our own unhealthy ways of dealing with things), but as I reflect back on that moment, I see that I wasn't actually choosing to care for myself but instead to get farther away from myself. To put it simply, by staying busy I was avoiding my own feelings of anxiety about the future I couldn't predict. So there I was, lost in my old and familiar coping mechanisms of dealing with uncertainty and discomfort by filling the empty spaces, distracting, and numbing. I managed to get my luggage, rent a car, buy a new purse and new sunglasses, have lunch, drink a glass of wine, and drive down the coast of sunny California all in a matter of an hour and a half . . . and yes, I was late arriving and feeling flustered.

So why was my coping mechanism of choice to stay busy and numb out? The simple truth . . . years and years of practice. Instead of sitting with the discomfort of my anxiety and uncertainty (which is all anxiety really is), I tried to dodge it. And just below the surface of my discomfort were thoughts like: "What will this be like . . . will I be accepted . . . will it hurt . . . will I feel too much, past the point of no return . . . what if I don't stop crying . . . what does it mean to ask these hard questions about myself, my past, and my future . . . will I be seen . . . will I still feel loved, even if I tell my truth, or change?" Damn. Those questions cut deep, and it's no wonder I wanted to push them down, ignore them, and pretend they didn't exist. Don't we all? But luckily, the leader and very gifted therapist in charge of the weekend invited me to let down my guard, to lean into my feelings, and assured me that, even when I dove headfirst into some of life's deepest waters, I would come up for air—a better kind of air. By the end of the weekend, after we all had gotten more comfortable with each other than we could have imagined (that's what a shitload of feeling your feelings and self-disclosure will do to you), I discovered that I wasn't alone in my feelings of uncertainty about what the experience would be like. Of course I wasn't alone in my feelings . . . we never are.

As vulnerable as it is to say, being a mental health professional and all, I have many more stories like the one I just shared . . . where I turned away from my feelings instead of toward them. While I still have to actively push back on my desire to bulldoze over my own feelings and put on a smile, I've come a long way since that weekend when I chose to surrender. Through my own self-work, therapy, and radical acceptance, I'm learning to allow myself to feel the loss of things I never chose to give away, the loss of certain hopes and dreams, the loss of friends and loved ones I held dear, and even the loss of my own babies who never made it into this world.

So while the relearning of how to feel my feelings started way back in graduate school and continued on my therapy retreat, it certainly didn't end there. It's a process, a journey really, that I'm (imperfectly) signed up for. Here's what I'm learning about feeling my own feelings: when I allow myself to feel all of my emotions, not just the pretty ones, but the messy and painful ones too, it hurts and at times I feel untethered but I also feel something distantly familiar . . . freedom. The weight of silence, the heaviness of holding other people's feelings and ignoring my own, and the stress of trying to blaze past the hurt melts from my shoulders and I can breathe deeper. I feel like I'm right back there on the ice, cutting through it with my blades, and skating my heart out . . . and even though I know I could fall flat on my face, I don't stop.

Why are so many of us avoidant of our feelings even though we know emotions are a natural part of life? For myself, and most of the people I've sat with in the therapy room, the answer is usually a combination of two things—we don't know how to feel our feelings (we were never taught, therefore we're out of practice), and we're threatened by them. We are threatened by our emotions because we've bought into the myth that if we allow ourselves to feel, the floodgates will open so wide that we'll drown in them. Here's another truth—feeling our feelings means breaking homeostasis (changing up the way we are used to doing things) and we humans often have a hard time with that. This is where it feels appropriate to say, "Old habits die hard." I'm not sure who said it originally, and I'm sure I could GTS (Google that sh**), but let me get back to my point, which is, change can feel really scary. I truly believe underneath the fear of feeling is this one simple and primal question: "But will I crumble . . . will it all come crumbling down?"

I'm here to tell you that you won't crumble . . . that, yes, it might feel uncomfortable, and even painful at times, BUT if you don't allow yourself to feel, process, and deal with your emotions the suffering will eventually come and it will hurt worse than you imagined. The suffering might come in the form of addiction, broken or unfulfilling relationships, missed opportunity, and/or the regret of a life not fully lived.

Bearing witness to people learning how to better cope with and move through their emotions in the name of less suffering comes with the territory of being a therapist, but it's also an incredible privilege. The way I see it, that's what therapy is all about . . . opening up space for feeling, processing, and dealing with the emotions that arise from your lived experience. And while I have many stories of guiding people through that kind of work, there is one in particular that stands out. Every client I've seen has impacted me in some way or another, but this client I'm going to share about has a story I'll never forget—a story of stuffing down her feelings so deep that they almost killed her, and a story of incredible healing and reclaiming.

Lucy was a grown woman, who came to me because she was experiencing what she described as panic attacks, for the first time ever. Soon you'll understand why. Lucy was a mother of four children, and she dedicated her life to helping others via nonprofit and social work. She was the youngest of seven children, raised by alcoholic parents, considered herself the "peacemaker" in her volatile home, and later ended up in a physically, sexually, and emotionally abusive marriage. When Lucy's children were out of the house, she got the courage and strength to leave her marriage and ended up remarrying a very kind and gentle man—whom, she proudly announced, she never (ever) fought with. So there she was, in my office, this beautifully dressed blond woman with a smile on her face, telling me, with no observable emotion, about her attempted suicide. She told me that just the other day, she was driving home from work and she became overwhelmed with feelings that she couldn't put into words, but they felt so bad that she imagined the only way out was death. She told me that she decided to drive her car off a cliff, but at the last minute she didn't. Instead, she went home and had dinner with her husband as though nothing had happened—she never told him or anybody else until she told me in that very moment.

She went on to tell me that this wasn't the first time she had felt suicidal, but she had never told anybody before and, for the sake of her children and grandchildren, she didn't want to die. I remember thinking (embarrassingly) something along the lines of, "Shit, I thought this was going to be an easy case" (yes, we therapists are human and have thoughts like that too). To be honest, I assumed she was just another middle-aged woman coming to me for help with the stress and overwhelm she felt in her life due to all of her family, career, and social undertakings—and not to say those things aren't real struggles, but they are usually pretty easily sorted out with some good therapy. I knew, after hearing that story and seeing the lack of affect (emotion) on her face or in her body language that there was going to have to be a lot of undoing and relearning to feel and deal so that she could, finally, heal. Lucy was living from the belief that her sole purpose in life was to serve and appease other people. She believed that there was no space for her to have negative emotion . . . because it wasn't safe (a belief often held by adult children of alcoholics or anybody who has experienced abuse), and since her needs were never met by her expressing her emotions as a child, why would they be now? Also, it was unclear whether or not she even knew how to name any emotion other than positive emotion, which no matter how many gracious acts she performed, or material things she acquired, she stopped feeling too. So I broke the news. I told her that she wasn't broken, but instead, she was incredibly resilient to have survived such hard things and that she was simply using a coping mechanism that kept her safe as a child and a young adult but no longer served her as a grown woman. All that stuffing down of feelings and giving away of herself was really just an undercover way for her to distract from pain. I was right—Lucy was incredibly resilient and in just a few months of therapy was starting to make big changes, including intentionally bringing up conversations with her husband that could cause conflict (yes, one of our therapy goals), saying "no" to people and events that didn't bring her joy, and sitting with her feelings of sadness and regret from her past. During our last therapy session together, I couldn't help but think, "There she is . . . there she is." That same beautiful and impeccably dressed woman who had entered my office months ago was finally showing up in her truth, and she moved so much more freely.

LET'S WORK TOWARD CHANGE . . .

So now that you've (hopefully) bought into the idea that it's critical to our well-being to feel our authentic feelings, you're probably wondering something along the lines of "Cool, but where do we go from here?" I often hear some version of this from my clients: "This whole letting myself feel thing sounds right, but how do I feel and what the hell do I do when I want to be done feeling?" I get it—life moves one way . . . forward. And most of you reading this book likely have a lot of moving parts—children, partners, loved ones, employers, or employees who depend on you being a functional human being, so you can't afford to let your feelings slow you down for too long. Before I invite you into a healthier way of feeling and dealing, I'm going to remind you of these two truths: 1. The cost of ignoring or blazing through your feelings will be SO much higher than the price of making room for them; 2. We are hardwired to feel and when we mess with that wiring, our system starts to malfunction, sending out alerts by way of physical illness, anxiety, anger, and more.

I don't know how you'll feel about this (no pun intended), but I know that the first time I learned about healthier ways to cope with my feelings I was pretty freaking annoyed. Here's why—the only way out is through; there is no shortcut when it comes to the process of learning how to cope with our emotions (a therapist I follow on Instagram, named Tiffany Roe, cleverly refers to this process as "feel, deal, heal"). Here's how it goes: something happens that triggers a physical sensation or emotion (usually both), and it's your job to give that feeling a name. Is it sadness, worry, overwhelm, fear, loneliness, exhaustion? Don't underestimate this part, because often we are so used to talking about our feelings via our thoughts that we can forget how to name our emotions. Do a little experiment for me—try asking somebody how they felt about something and notice that you'll likely get a response in which they share a thought they had about the situation instead of a feeling. Why? Because it's somehow much easier for us to stay up in our heads than it is to be in our bodies and with our feelings and inner knowing.

After we name our feeling/feelings, we do the hardest thing—we acknowledge the feeling, get curious about it, and then sit with it. We notice where we feel it in our body, pay attention to what it feels like, and what memories or past events it reminds us of, and then we let it be with us. We can even talk to it, and maybe it will go something like this: "Hi, anxiety, it's you again . . . I feel you in my chest and it feels hard to breathe with you here. When that thing just happened (insert experience here), it made me feel scared, and then I started imagining the worst-case scenario. You feel uncomfortable, but you're here with me." Lastly, after we've acknowledged it, gotten curious about it, and sat with it, we move through it. Pause for a second, because what I don't want you to hear is "we move past it." Nope, we move with it and through it.

There are a lot of different ways you can move with and through your feelings, and every person resonates with different ways of dealing—which is why I fully reject claims that there is one "perfect" solution when it comes to anything mental- or emotional-health related. Here are some choices around practicing sitting with and moving through your feelings (but remember, don't do what I often try to do, which is skip the steps that come before this one): you can take some deep breaths, you can have a good cry on the couch, you could meditate, go for a walk, dance, run, call a friend, schedule a therapy appointment, reevaluate your medication needs, journal, scream into a pillow, draw a picture, play with your kids, go for a hike, go for a drive, sit by the ocean, lie under a tree, plan for a new way forward . . . it doesn't matter what the "doing" part is, so long as it gives you a way to move through whatever big feeling you're experiencing. You know those tantrums your kid throws (or used to throw); that's them moving through their big, messy feelings, and while it presents a challenge for us parents, it's a reminder that we aren't meant to stuff our feelings, but instead to feel them, let them move through us and then out of us via expression! The good news is, we don't have to kick or scream our way through our feelings anymore, but instead we get to name them, listen to them, feel them, and act wisely from them.

What were you taught about feelings/emotion as a young child by your family of origin or other influential adults in your life?

What is your relationship with feeling your feelings like now? Do you allow yourself to feel them? Do you stuff, avoid, numb (eat, drink, shop), or distract? Maybe you're somewhere in-between, or maybe it's changed over time . . . all of it's OK, just be honest, and beware of going down the shame spiral here . . . none of us is perfect at feeling our feelings or therapy and self-help wouldn't have to exist!

What are you afraid would happen (if anything) if you were to allow yourself to fully feel and then express your feelings? I.e., "I'll never stop crying," or "nobody will get it," or "I'll feel worse," or "I'll be perceived as weak," or "I'll feel bad for a bit but better in the end."

Think of a time when you didn't express how you truly felt about something, and in turn you didn't get your own needs met and/or were let down. How might you have felt different if you expressed your feelings in the moment instead of stuffing them down?

Do you believe that the outcome would have been different if you had expressed your actual feelings? I.e., That one time I told my husband I wasn't upset about the choice he made to go to dinner with his friends, but inside I was feeling sad and let down and then later that week I exploded and we had a huge fight!

Feel, deal, heal! Pick one person or scenario you are going to practice sitting with your feelings with just a little bit longer. I.e., next time my kid tells me they are scared of something and it triggers my own feelings of anxiety, I am going to choose to sit with that feeling (instead of rush to fix it for them) and give them a big hug.

RESTORE

YOUR

AUTHENTIC

SELF

Chapter 4

YOU'RE INVITED TO FIND THE "WHY"

"I have learned that as long as I hold fast to my beliefs and values, and follow my own moral compass, then the only expectations I need to live up to are my own."

—MICHELLE OBAMA

When I'm working with people in therapy, regardless of their issues, circumstances, or history, one of the first things we do together is determine the "why" behind their efforts to grow, heal, or change. Finding our "why" is a critical part of the evolution process because it gives us the courage, strength, and fuel we need to keep going (imperfectly) even when things get hard. Most of us have more than one "why" in this life, but the common thread that I see among our "whys" is that we all want more freedom, space, and time to engage with the people and things that bring meaning and joy to our lives. People come to therapy, or do self-work, so that they can get unstuck . . . but a lot of people end up staying stuck. Why? Because, to keep it real, committing to changing the parts of ourselves that could use some changing is damn hard, and even downright painful sometimes. Yes, when we commit to doing self-work, we hope that we will be able to let go of the ways of thinking and behaving that are holding us back from living the best version of ourselves, but as my dad always said, "Old habits die hard." (P.s. in writing this book I came to find out it was actually Benjamin Franklin who said that . . . not my dad.) Regardless, though, he had a point—changing the beliefs and habits that are deeply ingrained in us is hard and not for the faint of heart.

If we don't have clearly in our sights what values are behind our desire to live better, we can easily lose traction or give up before the "magic" happens. In other words, in order to muster the courage to go beyond what we are used to, or what has been historically safe for us—we need a compelling reason . . . the big "why."

So how do we do the work of narrowing down our big "why"? We can start by determining our top values—and a really simple way to do this (which I'll lead you through at the end of the chapter) is to think about, when it's all said and done and you've left this world, how do you hope your loved ones will remember you? What impact do you hope to have left? Likely, you don't hope to be remembered as somebody who had a perfectly clean house, never rocked the boat, and followed the rules but never her own heart. I know, I know that sounds really depressing . . . but we have all had the experience of living out of line with our values and suffering for it. When we passively accept the values that have been handed down to us, or the ways of being that we have simply fallen into—we aren't living intentionally, and we certainty aren't in the driver's seat of our own life. As grown adults, we are the only ones who can decide what the hell REALLY matters most to us in life, and then give ourselves the permission to imagine what our life might look like if we choose to live with those things at the forefront.

The reason I chose Michelle Obama's words at the beginning of the chapter (other than the fact that she is one my own personal SHEROES) is because it points to the truth that when we put our own personal values at the forefront of our decision-making, we give ourselves the freedom of having to please nobody else in the world other than ourselves. When we're confused, lost, or uncertain we get to ask ourselves this one critical question (if you're a note taker, get out that highlighter, girl): "Is this choice moving me closer to or further away from my values?" If you were a boat drifting at sea, and you had a choice to either steer your boat toward a beautiful, warm island or leave it up to the water—chances are you'd grab the damn wheel. Determining our "why" (the island) allows us to be more willing to weather life's rough waters, because all the while we know we are moving toward our own true north (our values).

MY INVITATION IN . . .

So, what does all this values stuff look like in practice? I am going to let you in on my big "why," and then I'll walk backward through my own story to show you how I determined the three values that I've chosen to guide me through my imperfect journey of motherhood and beyond: freedom, connection, and joy. Let's start with my early motherhood journey (which I'm still technically in, but no longer head just above water). Becoming a mother narrows our vision so that we are able to keep our tiny humans alive and well. We are biologically hardwired to function in this way—and it's beautiful and symbiotic that our brains and bodies prioritize our babies' needs over our own. However, sometimes that constricted view sticks around a bit too long, or we're unsure how to widen our view and we end up losing sight of what's truly important. This is what I call "losing the plot." I think we all lose the plot from time to time, in different aspects of life, and for me, early motherhood was definitely one of those times.

Enter my first call to my current therapist, aka my plot changer. Before I go any further, I have to admit something. I (the therapist) had STILL only ever been to therapy once (yes, one session . . . during that whole breakup situation) before starting to see my current therapist. Remember how I told you earlier that I was always considered the fixer or the "solid" one . . . well, when we adopt titles like that sometimes we also dangerously adopt the belief that we can solve all of our own problems and we don't need help from anyone else. I overidentified with the role of "helper" until I was deep in the motherhood struggle. I made that first call to my therapist because I had the opportunity to hear her podcast, where she was brave enough to be vulnerable about her own struggles, and it made me feel safe enough to do the same. This is yet another example of the power of speaking our truth, because while we are doing it for our own healing journey, we have the potential to impact so many others who haven't yet ventured to use their voice.

I remember treading so lightly during that first session. As somebody who has always been good at reframing, or finding the positive, this new territory of feeling inept and even disgusted by myself felt unfamiliar. It was hard for me to admit that I was feeling overwhelmed, and not as joyful as I thought I should be in the role of motherhood. Wasn't being a "mom" SUPPOSED to make me blissful and grateful every moment? I mean, I was lucky enough to have an exceptional husband and father to my children, a career that I found meaning and success in, and three healthy children. Also, with the background I have in child development, shouldn't I know that yelling at my kids and shaming them is certain to land them in a lifetime of their own therapy? Minus the lack of sleep, I couldn't understand why little things, like dishes in the sink or a messy playroom (kind of the point of play-rooms) would send me over the edge. I often found myself getting unreasonably angry with the kids, raising my voice (OK, fine, yelling) and feeling like I was falling short of the mom I wanted to be. "Congratulations, you're human!" said my therapist (or something along those lines)—and I remember laughing and feeling relieved. The ironic thing is, in my professional life, I sat with countless women and told them some version of the same thing . . . but when it came to my own struggle, I couldn't seem to find the forest for the trees.

So there I was, feeling anxious and even depressed, putting so much more weight on what I was doing "wrong" than what I was doing right. Why? Because instead of parenting with my values at the forefront, I was parenting out of fear. Going a layer deeper (we therapists like to do that) I was allowing my unhelpful beliefs around being a "perfect" parent for my kids to stop me from being free to pursue true connection and joy. It wasn't like as soon as I connected those dots I never cared about a dish in the sink or a foiled plan again, but I was able to practice coexisting with the messiness of life so that I could make space for the things and moments that mattered the most to me. Before having kids, I don't think I felt pulled to think about my top life values. I just sort of lived in a way that made sense to me in the moment. I think it took getting lost in motherhood for me to actually do the work of discovering who I was as Kaitlin the woman, instead of Katie (the girl).

Here's what I've realized: it matters more to me that my kids notice me freely moving through life (not bound by the "should," or mindless rules set forth by others) than it does that things look perfect in my home or on Instagram. It matters more to me that we take the time to connect, via messy family dinners, adventures, or late-night pillow talks than it does that they get to bed at the perfect time. It matters more to me that we laugh, act silly, and celebrate one another than it does that we play by the rules. So there you have it: freedom, connection, joy—the three values that I chose in the beginning of my growth journey, and continue to choose, to lead the way when it comes to how I move through the world as "mom." As we move through different seasons of our life, the things we value most might change . . . so we have to remember to review, revisit, AND (sometimes) revise the stuff that matters the most to us!

I think it's important to say—I still mess up (often) and am reminded that I am acting out of line with my values, but I am able to apologize, change up my behavior, and move on. Case in point, just the other day my older daughter told me she thought she needed a break from our house. I wanted to blame it all on the pandemic and her not having been in school for over nine months, but that wouldn't be the whole truth. The whole truth is that I had just come off a particularly challenging day at work and was rushed and impatient with them at bedtime (OK, FINE, yelling) and she was taking on my stress, feeling unheard and overwhelmed. Now, before you go thinking that there's going to be a Hallmark moment next—don't worry, there wasn't. It took me the whole rest of the night to get out of my own head and realize the effects of my behavior on her before I was able to acknowledge it, apologize, and move on. She, as kids most always do, thanked me, gave me a hug, and moved on. Connection—check!

My commitment to myself on this mother journey is this: no more hiding in shame, no more suffering alone, no more anything but moving toward the direction of my own true north.

And speaking of my own true north, or my big "why" when it comes to parenting—truly, it's knowing that if I live my life with the values of freedom, connection, and joy at the forefront, my children will have permission (and be invited) to do the same.

YOUR INVITATION IN . . .

We typically don't sit around pondering our values, nor do we think we have the time or luxury to do so—until we find ourselves either in crisis or too close for comfort. That's often the way it works with mental health and personal growth . . . we don't seek it until we really "need" it—and if we want to change that archaic narrative it has to start with us.

Although I don't look back at my earliest years of motherhood, which are close in my rearview mirror, with regret—I do look back and wish I had reached out for help sooner. In my postpartum haze, which by the way lasts far beyond the six-week mark when your doctor gives you that dreadful green light to resume sexual activity, I couldn't see how stuck I was, or maybe even more important, that I needed to stop standing so stubbornly alone on my island of dread. I miss my kids' chubby baby hands, and the simplicity of the days spent at home, but I don't miss the sense of dread I felt around nap schedules and feedings, the dread I felt around the uncertainty of it all. Would I get five hours of sleep that night, or one? Were they throwing up my breast milk because of something I ate, or because their little systems were still developing? Is Army green REALLY a normal color for poop? OK, I digress—because now I'm giving myself a bit of PTSD just thinking of it all. Maybe you have a similar story, or maybe you don't, but most all of us have had the experience of living through a season when we felt lost, uncertain, or out of line with who we are and where we're headed.

In my professional work, I have seen so many brave souls do the work of imperfect evolution by choosing values-based living over fear-based living. Since one of my specialty areas is working with people who struggle with anxiety disorders, I end up working with a lot of women who have been diagnosed with obsessive-compulsive disorder (OCD). If there ever was a mental health disorder that tried to rob the joy out of the things you care most deeply about, OCD would be it. I have so many stories of brave women, men, and children doing the hard work of overcoming their OCD—and I'll share about one particularly brave client in a minute. But before I dive into our work together, I have to fill you in on a few facts about OCD, because it is a mental health disorder that is sorely misrepresented in popular culture, television, and movies. It is not simply about liking to be organized, clean, neat, or "anal." It is a mental health disorder that can be terrifying to live with, and often causes great disruption and pain in one's life when it's unrecognized and not properly treated.

To put it simply, OCD can be defined as a disorder that causes people to have unwanted and repetitive intrusive thoughts that cause a high level of fear and/or anxiety, which leads the person suffering from the disease to believe they need to do a physical or mental compulsion to get rid of that thought or keep the "bad" thing from happening. One of the most common and least talked about categories of OCD is often referred to as harm OCD—a type of OCD that is centralized around fears of harming yourself or somebody else. New postpartum mothers with a history of anxiety tend to be susceptible to developing OCD (or having an increase in symptoms), and for my client, Keri, that was the case. Note: Because worries of harming their own babies can be a part of OCD, new mothers with this condition might get misdiagnosed as having postpartum psychosis, a very serious (and more common than many think) mental health illness that needs immediate attention. Back to Keri . . . she dreamed of being a mother, she had a hard time getting pregnant, suffered a few miscarriages, and then, finally, had a successful pregnancy that gifted her a beautiful little boy. She had a history of anxiety but felt she had always managed well (which is short for swept it under the rug to attend to other people's needs).

In her first session, Keri told me with eyes full of tears and shaking hands, "I don't trust myself alone with my baby . . . I can't do this." My heart sank for her, because new motherhood, and the journey to get there, is hard enough without the added stress of OCD. When we first become mothers, I think most of us feel blindsided by how hard it actually is—but that's not what Keri meant. She went on to explain to me that whenever she was alone with her baby, she had images of accidentally smothering him, or drowning him in the bath, or dropping him down the stairs. She was terrified to tell me her truth, because she had never heard of this kind of OCD (harm) before and just assumed she was "going crazy." She had been to a therapist before me who suggested that she might be experiencing psychosis (aka going crazy), which further traumatized her and made her more afraid to speak the truth about her struggles.

She found her way into my office, and I knew right away that she was suffering from postpartum OCD. The true difference between somebody who is suffering from OCD versus somebody who is sociopathic or suffering from another mental health disorder is that they actually don't WANT to do the thing they're scared of doing . . . and the thought terrifies them so much they often avoid doing anything at all. For Keri, this looked like purposely avoiding her baby boy (when she could), putting her husband in charge of bath and diapering, and generally feeling incredibly disconnected from the baby she loved more than anything in the world. Again, being a new mom is hard enough, but for mothers suffering with postpartum depression, anxiety, or OCD, it feels almost impossible—trudging through deep, dark, and sticky mud.

The first part of treatment involved working with Keri to understand that she was not going crazy, and that while it's really unfair, it's common for OCD to target the parts of life you care about the most; and in this case, her ability to be the loving and present mother she was just underneath her thick layer of anxiety.

As the shame dissipated, we were free to jump into the second part of the work of therapy, which involved (you guessed it) determining her values and her own big "why." Her values, things like presence, family, and peace, were the fuel that would give her the energy to go down the road toward her big "why" of being able to show up as her truest and most loving self for her child. And fuel she needed, because as we all know, facing our fears is incredibly hard, but when it comes to treating OCD, and all types of anxiety, it's key to recovery. Keri was incredibly brave in doing the challenges set forth in therapy (technically referred to as Exposure and Response Prevention, which is a type of therapy aimed at helping people get used to and less triggered by feared thoughts and situations), including allowing herself to sit with whatever disturbing thoughts arose as she gave her child a bath, changed his diaper, and more. She eventually got better and started to enjoy the parts of motherhood that had felt impossible. Taking the time to discover her big "why," and a fearless commitment to move toward it, was ultimately her path out of despair. Truth be told—I think it's all of ours too.

LET'S WORK TOWARD CHANGE . . .

I invite you to take charge of your life, to get in that damn driver's seat so you can have a chance at traveling in the direction you hope your life will go. The COVID pandemic highlighted the truth that there is so little we are in control of in life and that maybe the ONLY thing that is certain is uncertainty itself. So while discovering our values and then committing to live by them (to the best of our ability) is critical work—it doesn't guarantee an easier road, but instead a more intentional one. Perhaps the biggest and most important truth when it comes to our emotions is that we aren't able to selectively feel. In other words, we don't get to decide to feel only the positive emotions—we have to feel ALL the feelings in order to feel the good stuff. This is why recovering alcoholics and addicts often talk about the experience of being sober and feeling a wider range of emotions than ever before because in their attempts to numb out the difficult feelings, they numbed out the positive ones too.

In order to truly live in line with our values, or our "why," we need to be open to feeling all the big feelings (sadness, pain, joy, uncertainty, fear) that might come our way . . . there's just no way around it. BUT we will do so knowing, all the while, that we are living a life we choose—a life full of unexpected storms, twists, and turns, but a life steered by our own conviction.

What actually matters to you in the long run? Yes, this is an open-ended question on purpose . . . but if you need more direction think about this: when you're lying on your deathbed (hopefully after a long, fulfilling life) and it's all said and done—what impact do you hope you will have made on your loved ones or the world?

Taking your answer to the previous question into consideration, what would you say is most important or valuable to you? Is it being a "kind and loving" parent/friend/partner? Is it living a life full of adventure and fun? Is it being a helper or change-maker in the space of your career/life's work? Whatever it is . . . write it out here.

Write down your "why" for wanting to work on your own personal growth. Remember, we have "whys" in the realm of parenting, career, family, spirituality, community, and more . . . but for this exercise, let's just focus on your "why" for committing to your own growth. If you need direction, try completing this sentence: "I am committed to growing and evolving because it will allow me to experience more (blank) and feel more (insert emotion here)."

Chapter 5

YOU'RE INVITED TO CHALLENGE YOUR NARRATIVE

"You either walk inside your story and own it or you stand outside your story and hustle for your worthiness."

—BRENÉ BROWN

Excuse my lack of sophistication while I say, this is where shit gets really real. Challenging our narrative (or as Brené Brown says, "the stories we tell ourselves") is both hard and powerful . . . it's the heart of change work. Getting curious about our narrative (the things we tell ourselves) and then gaining the courage to call ourselves on our own bullshit is both hard AND freeing! Now that we've reflected on and gotten the chance to understand our story a bit better (in Chapter 1), we are invited to do the work of challenging the beliefs we've come to hold about ourselves, or the world, that don't actually serve us and our growth process. Why? Because we know that our unhelpful narrative, made up of total bullshit thoughts, acts as a roadblock for us moving toward our "big whys" in life. At the risk of saying basic, I'll just say this—our limiting beliefs do nothing but limit us, and we're not here for it anymore. We are going to talk about how to challenge and expand our narratives so that we can "take back the wheel" from our storytelling minds, but first we need to better understand what limiting beliefs are and how in the hell we ended up with them.

When we aren't functioning well, or find ourselves stuck in spaces that no longer fit, it's likely because our limiting (yes, bullshit) beliefs are taking the mic, so to speak, and getting ALL the airtime—running the show.

Now, the good news (or bad, depending on how you look at it) is that we're not fully responsible for these bullshit stories we tell ourselves. To better understand how to change the relentless cycle of our limiting beliefs getting too much real estate in our brains, we need to understand a little bit about two of the main ways we form the beliefs that become our narrative (often called inner script): 1. Through the things we were/are told about ourselves; and 2. Through our experience and environment.

THE THINGS WE WERE TOLD ABOUT OURSELVES (IMPLICITLY AND EXPLICITLY)

Let's start with the fun one—all the ways our parents and loved ones messed us up. Just kidding—kind of. I am only kind of kidding because for all the ways they may have contributed to our limiting beliefs, we want to keep in perspective that it may be that many of the things we learned from them were helpful and protective too. Both things are true. The fact is, the thoughts that most frequently run through our head are informed by the beliefs we formed in childhood through things that were either implicitly (not through words but through action) or explicitly (through words and actions) told to us by the people in our life that were most influential.

Let's start with the things that were implicitly told to us—these can be the hardest to uncover. As it turns out, your parents' words, feedback, and responses to you mattered—a whole hell of a lot.

Let's go way back to your first experience with learning. Were you the kid who carefully colored in the lines and sat quietly, or were you the kid who colored outside the lines and cared more about chatting with your buddies than listening to the teacher? Well, maybe you were sometimes both version of that kid . . . but the truth is, you were likely categorized as one or the other by something somebody said about you, or their response to you. For example, if you overheard your teacher telling your mom something along the lines of: "Sara (let's be real—if you're reading this you know a lot of Saras) is really struggling with following directions, she's messy, and often off-task." Let's assume that the teacher was trying to be helpful, but all your five-year-old brain heard was "I am not very good at school, I'm not like the others." With a few repeat experiences, Sara had frequent thoughts of "bad, or failed," which, sadly, helped her form the belief that she was "not enough, and not worthy."

I'm going to throw a curveball here, because the example I just shared is obviously harmful—but there are other implicit messages that are a bit more subtle. Let's use Jenny (you knew Jennys too)—the girl who LOVED to color, and prided herself on staying in the lines, following directions, and reading out loud in class. Sounds fabulous, right? Jenny often got praise when she did things "perfectly," or "beautifully," and was considered to be at the top of her class, academically and socially. Jenny had frequent thoughts like, "When I am careful, cautious, good, and always doing the 'right' thing, then I get attention." The collection of these thoughts added up to form the belief that she needed to be perfect to be worthy of love. As life threw its stuff at Jenny, as it does, it became impossible to keep up with her own standards of perfection—and she often felt the need to perform and hide her true feelings, which led to feelings of anxiety and depression.

Explicit beliefs—those are a bit easier to uncover and connect the dots from the experiences we had to the beliefs we then formed. When we are young and our trusted people tell us things like "you are bad at math," "sports just aren't your thing," "you're a liar," or "you are always so sensitive," we are of course going to believe those things about ourselves.

The bottom line is, whether we are Jennys or Saras, children are programmed to believe what they are told about themselves. As children, we often don't yet have the tools needed to balance the (shitty or not fully true) stories we are told about ourselves with other and more protective stories—we believe what our parents tell us because that's what we know to be true within the framework we are working in. If some version of one of these stories resonates with you (maybe with a different implicit message)—it's very likely that same theme has been on repeat throughout your life (starting in childhood) and reinforced through your experiences as an adolescent and an adult. And when we choose to keep believing the things we were once told about ourselves because we don't know anything different, we can't possibly be the best version of ourselves—or even know what that looks like, for that matter!

But here's what is also true and important to understand: we are now grown adults, and we get to make the choice whether or not we want to continue to believe the shitty things we have come to believe about ourselves and abilities, or whether we're ready to grab our life by the balls (actually, ovaries) and flip the script. I am not saying it will be easy, or perfect, but you already know that by now.

MY INVITATION IN . . .

Let me share a story with you about uncovering two of the most impactful limiting beliefs I've held over the years, the events that inspired me to challenge them, and what expansive beliefs I'm working on embodying.

LIMITING BELIEF: "MY SELF-WORTH IS TIED TO THE SHAPE OF MY BODY."

Let's start with a limiting belief that I adopted when I hit puberty, grew curves, and got diagnosed with a thyroid disorder all at the same time—"My self-worth is tied to the shape of my body." I know that I'm not the only one who has struggled with this belief—and as adult women, most of us now believe that beauty comes in many different shapes, sizes, and skin colors. When we were young girls, however, we were likely much more susceptible to the implicit and explicit messages we heard about what it looked like to be beautiful. We were supposed to be thin, muscular (but not too muscular), tall (but not too tall), tan-skinned (but not too dark), athletic (but still feminine), smart (but not too opinionated), kind (but not at the risk of our popularity), confident (but not too needy), and the list goes on. These cultural and societal expectations don't live in a rule book anywhere, but that's because they don't need to—we know them by heart. We know them through what we're told, how we're watched and treated, what types of accomplishments are seen as worthy of celebration, and how we're depicted in stories.

Even though I was an athlete throughout high school and my body helped me accomplish some pretty cool things, I wasn't proud of how my body looked, and I did my best to hide what I thought were my "flaws" and awkwardly flaunt what I thought was my only asset (my boobs). When I look back at pictures now, I realize how ridiculous the notion was that I was "fat," but high school seems like the biggest breeding ground for insecurity. With Top Ten hottest lists, and I can't even imagine what it's like NOW with things like Snapchat and Instagram. Back to my story. (Have I told you yet that I have a bit of ADHD with my anxiety? Not yet, but we'll get there.) Friendships with boys always came easy to me, and so I spent a lot of time hearing them chat about all kinds of things, including which girl was a ten or a seven, and who wasn't even on their radar (gross, I know, but this was well before the "me too" movement and during a time where the rhetoric of "boys will be boys" was commonplace). One particular day, my best guy friend and I were having a conversation and he said something along the lines of, "The perfect girl would have your personality and her (referring to a blond and thin girl we were friends with) looks." Ouch. I pretended it didn't hurt, but my heart sank. I don't remember the exact thoughts that followed, but I imagine they were—"I'm not thin enough, pretty enough . . . anything enough." Yes, total bullshit, but I was fifteen, and I didn't have the ability or insight to challenge the culture's narrative of beauty. So I carried the story well into my later teens, took diet pills, and sometimes too easily gave away parts of myself (figuratively) to try to prove my worth.

What inspired me to put the middle finger to my belief that my self-worth was tied to the size of my body? A few things, but mostly . . . childbirth. There is nothing like childbirth, no matter how it happens, to show you the incredible power of your own body. It was messy, painful as all hell, but at the end of it—we (my body and I) gave birth to a child . . . three times!

The experience of childbirth, the experience of feeling every fiber in my body working to bring life into the world, made me feel like a warrior—like a mother. It's not that I never struggle with negative thoughts about the way I look in a picture (we all know to blame it on the angle), it's that I no longer get it twisted. I no longer believe that the size of my thighs and my self-worth have anything to do with each other. So here it is, the expansive belief I am living into: "My body is so much more than its size, my body can do amazing things, my body is for me." Do you see how there is so much more room in that belief than the old one? I don't get it perfect, that's for sure, but the expansive belief about my body allows me to be fully and unapologetically me.

Because I've worked through my own "stuff" when it comes to body image and self-worth, I am so intentional and mindful about the way I talk about the female body with my children (daughters and son). I don't talk badly about my body, I don't avoid being naked in front of them, I don't label foods as "good or bad." I am going to be really direct here. As a mental health professional, and a human being who experienced shame about my body (maybe you did too), I hope you'll be intentional when it comes to the topic of body too—our children are always watching and learning from us. While we can't shield them from most of the bullshit beliefs that the world puts out there about beauty and body, we sure as hell can show them what it looks like to focus less on what our body looks like and more on the amazing things it can do.

I'm going to hit you with another limiting belief I've struggled with and maybe you'll identify with it too: "Now that I'm a mother, pursuing my big dreams can only be done so long as it doesn't inconvenience them."

Becoming a mom is the most all-encompassing, and let's be real, insane experience. Before our little amoebas came into the world, there was literally no way we could fathom the love we would hold in our hearts for them, or the challenges they would come with. Keeping tiny humans fed, content (ish), cared for, and well is really hard—maybe the hardest job in the world. When we are postpartum and deep in the early season of motherhood there is almost no space for anything other than meeting their basic needs, let alone our own. We learn real quick, and maybe for the first time ever, that our needs no longer matter as much as theirs. And it's true—they need us to stay alive. I can picture my hot mess self in that season like it was yesterday—with two babies under two, dirty yoga pants, unwashed hair, piles of laundry, sore nipples, and feeling depleted and exhausted. My purpose was simple—keep those babies alive and well. But it's called postpartum (which, by the way, lasts for two years, NOT six weeks) because it's a season, a season that should eventually change. We aren't meant to stay in survival mode.

So what happens when we are ready (or not) to leave the house without the kids and pursue our life beyond "mom"? Guilt. Guilt happens. Even right now, as I type these words on this very page, I have twinges of guilt that I am staying home to write, instead of going to the zoo with the kids and their (very) loving and capable father. I sometimes find myself trying to squeeze work in early in the morning or late at night partly because life is freaking full but ALSO because . . . guilt. I have done a lot of work when it comes to giving myself permission to be more than mom, but I still struggle with the thoughts and feelings that come up when I take time for dreams, my body, my creativity, my spirituality, and my sense of self. Letting go of the limiting beliefs that fuel our mom guilt is a work in progress—I won't give up, if you don't either.

We have to reject the idea that when we are pouring into ourselves, we are taking from our children or partners. The belief I am working on stepping into, the more expansive belief, is: "When I take care of myself, and pursue my own hopes and dreams, I am a better human . . . I can both love them well and have a life beyond them."

YOUR INVITATION IN . . .

So here we are—now that I've shared personal examples of what the process of shifting from my own limiting beliefs to more expansive beliefs has looked like for me—I want to invite you to do the same. At the end of the day, I think we all want to talk to ourselves in ways that are more kind, helpful, and just less shitty . . . we recognize that we NEED to do this in order to have successful relationships, careers, etc., but where in the hell we start is what can feel so confusing! The notion, shared often by people who are trying to sell us something, that there is a quick fix that will solve all of our biggest problems and remove all the barriers is unhelpful, impractical, and just not true. The falsities we're often fed about personal growth can make us go down a shame spiral when we're less than #positivevibes only. You know it by now, but this isn't a fairy tale—life is messy, and we have to be gritty, willing, and able to keep coming back to the drawing board when life throws its myriad experiences and struggles our way.

What I mean is, once you learn the skill of discovering and changing the unhelpful beliefs that keep you small (which we'll dive into more in a minute), I want you to know something—you're going to screw it up. You are going to revert back to your old negative beliefs from time to time, maybe even a lot of the time, and feel bad about it. But here's the cool part, the life-changing part: you're going to NOTICE it's happening and have the opportunity to change your inner script and then whatever action might follow. You're going to find yourself. (One of my favorite questions I pose to my clients is, "Wait, whose story is this I'm carrying . . . does it belong to me or somebody else?") The most empowering moments in life are the ones where we finally decide to stop holding the weight that was never ours to hold in the first place. If you're in a particularly hard season or having a for-the-record-books rough day—it's going to be a hell of a lot harder to quiet that negative voice filling your head, like an unwanted houseguest, and that's OK. It's #realife.

You've already heard me talk a bit about expansive beliefs, but let's dive into it a bit more, so you can try it on for size. Expansive belief systems (what we want to develop) start with noticing that you're telling yourself a story, accepting that your mind is capable of telling all kinds of tales, and then deciding to live into a different story—one that is more in line with your values and the way you want to live your life in the right-now moment. The idea of expansive beliefs sits so much better with me, and most of my clients too, than does the idea of positive beliefs. Expansive thinking is NOT positive thinking. Expansive thinking helps us get unstuck from the limited (and shitty) beliefs that are holding us back and make MORE space for us to grow. You know me by now, and you know that I have an especially hard time (and you probably do too) with the whole "just be positive" concept. The truth is, we've all probably tried the whole toxic positivity thing, but here's the problem—we don't get to choose our damn emotions, or many of the things that happen to us in life for that matter, so we're only left with how we respond. Insisting that we think only positive thoughts or allow #goodvibes only is harmful because it makes us fall out of line with our actual human experience, driving us further away from our own feelings and experiences, and those of the people we love too.

Expansive beliefs are spacious and DRIVEN by our values. They function to move us toward the direction we hope to go in life . . . more peace, more calm, more adventure, more (insert your own version of more here). Expansive beliefs are the opposite of limiting beliefs; instead of making our world smaller, they allow for an opening up of opportunity and possibility—they make our world bigger.

How do we do it? I am going to leave an exercise at the end of this chapter to help you move through the process of creating more expansive beliefs using your own story—but here's how it works. You might have to read this part a couple of times before it makes sense; I'm going to do my best to break this down in a way that resonates without using all kinds of fancy and unnecessary psychology words. A triggering event happens, we have some automatic thoughts about that event, those thoughts bring on big emotions, and then we take action based on those thoughts and feelings, and most of the time that action isn't in our best interest (numb, avoid, distract, fight, flight, freeze). The automatic thoughts we have when a triggering event happens are informed by the limiting beliefs we were just talking about (the ones that we formed from the bullshit things we were told about ourselves or experiences we had). So while we can't change our automatic thoughts (they literally just pop up in our brains and are beyond our control), we CAN pause and take a moment to ask ourselves this question: "Is that thought really true? Even if it might be a true thought, is it helpful? Is it serving me in moving toward the life direction I intend to head to?" The answer is likely a simple "nope"! This is where we can create a more expansive belief—not a positive belief, but something that leaves more space for us to move toward our values.

Let me tell you how this mind-set shift (that's really what this is all about) worked, in real life, for one of my clients. In treating anxiety disorders, I work with a lot of incredibly gifted people who battle with the double-edged sword of perfectionism. As we know, people who are perfectionistic tend to be high achievers, but they also tend to suffer a great deal when they feel they have done anything less than perfectly—having a hard time separating who they are from what they do.

In order to prove her worthiness (something that we shouldn't have to prove) my client Gabby felt there was no room for mistakes in motherhood, relationships, or her job. She took very little risk, stayed in a job that made her miserable, all out of fear that trying something new would make her susceptible to criticism and judgment. Her limiting mind-set sounded something like this: "Mistakes, judgments, and criticism are a sign that I am not good enough or have failed." So of course, I did the therapist thing and asked her to identify one thing that she would do if we could wave the magic wand and get rid of her fear of failure or criticism. She said she had always wanted to paint, but she never tried because she remembered struggling with art as a kid. "Perfect," I said (ironically), and I challenged her to attend one of those moms'-night-out painting nights. We decided that if she was going to go, she was going to need to cut the bullshit and practice some expansive thinking. The motto/expansive thought she came up with was: "When I take a risk, there is opportunity for growth and I can cope with the judgments or criticism because I value growth more than perfection." And she went to that painting night, more than once, and didn't love the feeling she got when she saw other paintings that were clearly better than hers—but she did, indeed, choose to value her own growth MORE than her need to be perfect. And as she continued to do small brave things, using her expansive thoughts as fuel, she learned that it wasn't actually true that perfection was the only thing that made her worthy or lovable. She learned that she was worthy, just because she was worthy.

What we often get wrong about growth and change is that it has to happen in big or grandiose ways—in the form of long retreats, extreme diets, or even weekly therapy. I am going to call (you guessed it) bullshit on that. Maybe we do need weekly therapy, or to change our diet, or go on a retreat, but, from what I've seen, the thing that creates real and lasting change are the seemingly small but also really brave things we do to challenge our limiting beliefs on a daily basis. I want to invite you into the truth that you are worthy and allowed to challenge and change your narrative.

Think of a life event/situation that brought up big feelings (anxiety, fear, sadness, shame, anger) and write a bit about the situation here:

What negative automatic thoughts (things that came into your brain right away . . . if you're not sure, imagine what they might have been) did you experience?

What feelings/emotions/sensations did that event trigger?

What did you do in response to those feelings? Did that action move you closer to, or further away from, your values?

Looking back, what could you tell yourself that is more helpful or takes into account a fuller perspective?

Lastly, what "wiser" action could you have taken if you took that new, more balanced thought/perspective to heart?

The Practice

Chapter 6

YOU'RE
INVITED TO
WELCOME
UNCERTAINTY

"Fear is often our immediate response to uncertainty. There's nothing wrong with experiencing fear. They key is not to get stuck in it."

—GABRIELLE BERNSTEIN

Uncertainty and change—even just writing those words brings up some level of anxiety for me. Uncertainty is everywhere around us, and it often feels like the only thing certain in life is uncertainty itself. It's a part of life that we can't escape, and very few of us actually enjoy being uncertain. In fact, most of us have a strong disdain for uncertainty, and if we could, we would gladly do away with the reality of it. Uncertainty is the culprit for most all of our feelings of anxiety and angst; it's the current that carries our worry and also keeps us stuck. Uncertainty is what anxiety lives and thrives on—the threat of the unknown, the unfixable, and the unforeseen.

Introduce me to somebody who claims to "love" uncertainty (beyond roller coasters, traveling to an exotic destination, or starting a venture) and I promise I will call their bluff. Why? Because for the sake of our safety, we are biologically programmed to want and need to know what's next, or what we're up against, so to speak. Our primal brains have a strong need to know the outcome, which is why we often fight change EVEN when we know good may come of it. While our internal threat system's job is to be sensitive to uncertainty, and ultimately keep us safe, we humans are also highly adaptable to change. So the problem isn't that we can't handle change or uncertainty, but instead that we lack a belief in our ability to handle life's twists and turns.

LETTING GO OF THE ILLUSION THAT LIFE IS CERTAIN . . .

Letting go of the illusion that we can be certain about (really) anything in life means relinquishing the belief that we are in control . . . and that is scary. As I write this chapter it's February 2021, and we are still very much in the midst of a global pandemic in which moment to moment, and day to day, things are in flux, changing, and sure as shit, REALLY uncertain. Will our kids get to stay in school? If so, when? What does that mean for childcare? Will I have a job? Should I put my dream on hold to be home with them more often? Ugh, that sounds freaking horrible . . . but I probably should, right? That's what the "good" moms would do. Should we book that trip or wait? Should we see my parents or not? We are living in a space in time where we were collectively, and globally, the most uncertain we've ever been.

While the COVID-19 pandemic has acted as a massive highlighter for uncertainty—the truth is, it has surrounded us throughout our life and will continue to so long as we live. So while it may be hard for us (me included) to deal with the practice of learning to sit with and welcome uncertainty, it may be the most important skill we could learn when it comes to our evolution and growth.

Why should we learn to welcome uncertainty if it's such a damn hard thing to do? I'm not going to feed you the "all things worthwhile take effort" line, but I am going to tell you this truth—nothing in life will ever be completely certain. Not one thing. Yet think about the amount of time and energy we exhaust searching for answers, or trying to find ways to make life more predictable in order to avoid feeling afraid, or being uncomfortable, or experiencing suffering. When we demand that life be predictable, or expect that we will always be safe or pick the "right" choice, we cause ourselves to suffer, time and again.

Seeking certainty doesn't make you flawed; it makes you human—as I mentioned before, we are biologically wired to avoid things that have an unknown outcome. It's this wiring that is responsible for keeping us alive, helping us avoid situations that might have terrible outcomes. Do you remember that moment in the movie *Speed* when Keanu Reeves had to figure out which wire to pick in order to make sure the bus didn't explode? Terrifying (and if you were a tween in the '90s you were likely a Keanu Reeves fan too). That was such a memorable moment for us viewers because we can all relate to the intense fear that can come with not knowing what the outcome of our choice will be. Luckily, most of our decisions won't result in causing a bus to explode—but dealing with uncertainty can trick our brain into responding as though there is real and imminent threat.

The daily doses of uncertainty that we are given just by being alive are often hard to swallow. I gave some examples earlier of the types of anxious and uncertain thoughts the pandemic brought up for many of us, but (beyond pandemic) they can show up in our brain sounding like: "Should I stop breastfeeding? Should I really pursue a new career in my late thirties (as though there is an expiration date for your potential!)? If I take that leap, will my family approve? What if that headache is something more than just my sinuses acting up? Should I say yes to that invite, or make an excuse? Will this school be supportive for my kiddo? Which direction should I go?" I mean . . . I could go on, and on, and on with the litany of questions related to uncertainty that our brain serves up every day—but I digress because I want to get to the good news. The good news is, we can learn to override this need for certainty by changing our relationship with it—it takes some work, but I have my own story, and the stories of many of my clients, to prove it's doable, and life-changing.

Let me tell you one of my (many) stories of being in a tug-of-war with uncertainty and how I ultimately learned to let go. By "letting go" I mean practicing what I preach, so that I could loosen my grip around the need to know (control). Just like anything else that challenges us to self-reflect, reach out for some help, and then make a change, the process of learning to welcome uncertainty was not, and still is not, an easy one for me—but the benefit of being able to step back into the parts of my life that matter the most outweighs the cost of discomfort that comes with leaning in.

MY INVITATION IN . . .

I have to be honest, writing this chapter has been the easiest so far, because historically my resistance to things that are uncertain has been high. I am not someone who needs to know life's every next move, in fact I really enjoy spontaneity and trying new things. However, when it comes to experiencing physical sensations that I can't explain, I get majorly triggered—health anxiety is a real thing for me that comes and goes . . . and I notice my worry about my health increases when other things in my life are out of balance (i.e., I'm working too much, not sleeping well, not eating well, and not moving my body well). Also, there's nothing like a global pandemic to trigger the hell out of people who worry about their health. The need to be certain about our health is NOT unusual (about half of the clients I've ever worked with share this sentiment), but it had never affected me like it did in this past year. Thanks to my own therapy, years of studying and practicing anxiety treatment, and the pressure cooker that was the pandemic, I now understand that my health anxiety is really just one of the ways my body is trying to send me a message. When things feel out of control in any aspect of my life, I go straight into "overfunction" and "overproductive" mode in order to avoid my real feelings, but since our bodies are incredibly intuitive, they don't allow us to keep running from our feelings for long without sending us a signal. So our bodies act up not just for the sake of being jerks, but because we're not listening to what they're trying to tell us . . . which for me (and in the case of 2020) was simply, "Slow your roll, girl."

Here's how it goes for me: feel uncertain > triggers my anxiety > think about all the things I can't control > triggers more anxiety > go into avoidance mode via overproductivity > my physical sensations get loud > triggers more anxiety > think, "I think I might be dying." This either sounds completely ridiculous to you or 100 percent relatable. If you've been unlucky enough to experience panic attacks (women are twice as likely to get them as men) you know how terrible they can feel, but you may have NOT known that what often lies beneath them is the fear of things that are unpredictable. Once we have a panic attack, we might start to obsess over whether or not it means we're dying, or whether we'll have one again, where we'll be when it happens the next time, and who might see us/judge the hell out of us. Yes, I am an anxiety specialist who freaking has anxiety.

But let me tell you about the experience that I vividly remember, sitting on the floor of our bedroom on March 12', 2020, when the uncertainty shitstorm of the COVID-19 pandemic hit home. We had just started to hear the news that the virus was all over California and were going to go on a "short" (so naïve we were) lockdown in order to control the spread. But then again, the reality of a global pandemic was not something we could have ever known without having experienced it before. So what did I do? I went into total go mode: canceled our spring break plans in between the six virtual sessions with clients I held that day, rented a cabin in Tahoe because I wanted to mitigate the kids' sad feelings about canceling Disneyland—all while managing a fever and sore throat. "Moms don't have time to get sick," I told myself (what a crock of shit) and I kept on going.

We left for Tahoe the next day, I ignored my feelings of sickness (which were luckily fairly mild) and, like you, watched helplessly as the world as we knew it started to unravel. As we were in Tahoe, sitting at an empty resort full of snow and nobody else, I remember feeling this sense of persistent worry. I couldn't ignore the way my body was feeling anymore, and I started to have intrusive thoughts about having COVID-19 and dying. We know that many people did in fact die of COVID, but whether or not I actually had it (we still don't know) I was far from gravely ill. I had mild symptoms of COVID and MASSIVE symptoms of panic. While we were in Tahoe, I felt I was just going through the motions—as though I were watching a movie of my life unfolding but not really in the movie. The kids would play in the snow, I would smile and take a picture . . . but all I could feel was a sense of fear and doom.

For months after that trip, and as we stayed locked down in our home, I would lie awake at night feeling like I couldn't breathe, having to run to the bathroom with stomach issues, and just praying for the morning light to

Uncertainty is the culprit for most all of our feelings of anxiety and angst; it's the current that carries our worry and also keeps us stuck.

come, because that's when I would be able to think more rationally. I still saw twenty clients a week, tried to manage Zoom school (luckily with my husband and the help of my family), and just pushed through until I decided enough was enough. I missed my sleep. On top of it, how long was I going to preach to my clients and seventy-five podcast listeners (lol) about self-care before I took care of my own self? I didn't like the way it felt to be moving so far away from the things I most valued, like presence with my kids, and laughter and spontaneity in the name of fear of uncertainty.

After realizing that I was trying to use the same tools that I teach my own clients and still suffering a ton—I decided it might be time to consider some medication. Enter Lexapro. For me, taking a small dose of that magical pill/ SSRI (which is often used to treat both anxiety and depression) allowed me to better engage with my helpful thoughts and take the actions I needed to take to move toward my values. I want you to read that last sentence again . . . because medication isn't magical in that it takes away all your struggle, but it sometimes is the catalyst that ALLOWS you to do the "work" you need to do to feel better. I started sleeping again, exercising again, was more patient, less irritable with my kids, and when I did experience panicky feelings, I was more willing to just hang out with them instead of obsessively trying to get rid of them (fix, solve, avoid). The topic of medication for our mental health is controversial—and it shouldn't be. Fun fact: research widely shows that the best-practice treatment for anxiety disorders is therapy paired with medication. I am a CBT therapist (thought to be the most effective type of therapy for anxiety disorders) and I believe in the power of it wholeheartedly—but it wasn't enough for me.

It wasn't until the first time it was my turn to try the psych meds that I realized I too carried stigma around the topic. The belief that I "should" be able to deal with my intense anxiety on my own, without the help of medication (and especially as an "expert" and all), brought up feelings of shame and defeat. I told only a few trusted people that I was taking medication, and having honest conversations about my reservations and feelings of shame was helpful . . . but the thing that put my shame to bed the most was actually FEELING BETTER (the meds working). Now I tell everyone who wants to know, or who I feel inclined to tell (including my clients), and here I am telling you, reader, that I probably don't know, that I'm on psych meds. I do this because I want to be a part of breaking the stigma around taking medication for psychological health . . . because the stigma is real, and the stigma is harmful. Most of us wouldn't hesitate to take medication for a physical condition if we knew it was going to greatly improve the quality of our life, so why do we feeling so ashamed when it comes to taking medication for our mental health that can ALSO greatly improve our quality of life? Stigma—I hear it come up multiple times a week (and sometimes a day) when I talk to my clients about taking medication. We were told (by society, and maybe our families of origin) that psych meds are for people who are broken, or "other," and we, especially as moms, should just grin and bear the pain. I am not saying that medication is the answer to our psychological health—that's not true even by a long shot—but just like therapy, it can be a helpful part of us getting back to health and greatly improve our functioning and our lives.

I don't know whether I'll be on medication forever, but I do know I'm thankful that it gives me the space and freedom to be more present and less afraid—to better coexist with all the uncertainty that comes with the pandemic and beyond. When I'm feeling uncertain or afraid of what's next, I do three things: tell myself that it's a gift to care about my life and my loved ones so much that I'm this afraid of losing them, remind myself that I can't control what happens next, and invite myself to come back into the moment I'm in (to be right where my feet are).

YOUR INVITATION IN . . .

We all have different circumstances or life events that trigger our fear of uncertainty and ultimately our struggle to reckon with the truth that we have control over so few things in life. It's vulnerable to make space and room for uncertainty, takes a lot of practice and calls for a lot of grace. Your stories around dealing with uncertainty might be different than mine, but they're undoubtedly a part of your story. What I learned the most from my own battle with anxiety is that I need to give myself a lot more space for grace. I need to be kinder to myself. I haven't always been so good at giving myself grace . . . and I know I'm far from alone in that. In my one-on-one work with hundreds (or maybe even thousands) of women and men alike, I can say that we are universally challenged when it comes to being kind to ourselves.

Even with a graduate degree, a few fancy certificates, some meds, and a lot of my own self-work I, just like you, waver when it comes to my ability to welcome uncertainty. Our ability to allow space for the unknown will ebb and flow, but as long as we are willing to continue welcoming it—we are moving in the right direction.

Remember how I said we as humans are far more adaptable to change than we recognize? Well, this is the part where we're going to work on bolstering your belief in your ability to move with the ebb and flow of life. What does welcoming uncertainty actually look like in practice? It looks like loosening our grip around how we think things "should be" or how things "might turn out," and making room for all the possibilities and unknowns. It looks like living from a place that is led by our values, not by our fear. It looks like practicing mindfulness by allowing ourselves to be present in the moment as opposed to traveling back to the past or forward to the future (the places that anxiety LOVES to live in).

I have had the honor of watching so many brave souls go to battle with their fear of uncertainty. The perfect example? One of my clients, a forty-year-old woman named Kate was highly anxious and always avoided driving on freeways out of fear of all the bad things that could happen. She would imagine car accidents, suffering from a panic attack on the freeway with her kids in the car, and just about every scary thing associated with driving. Because of where she lived, this meant she rarely left the house and wasn't able to attend events important to her (kids' games, weddings, social gatherings, etc.). We started slowly by practicing what we call imaginal exposures (imagining scary things happening and then sitting with the emotions that come up without trying to get rid of them) and moved toward driving together on the freeway. Once Kate recognized all the beautiful things her fear of uncertainty was threatening to take from her—like time and memories with her loved ones—she was all in on learning to welcome uncertainty, even though it was hard! She still struggles with practicing welcoming but because she knows it allows her to live more freely, she keeps on going.

Have you ever heard the acronym for fear? False Evidence Appearing Real. Just the other day, I was on a beautiful hike and I saw what I thought was a snake, but turned out to be a lizard. Before I could even give my brain the "all clear," my body was in flight mode. I did this weird jump/ hop move, my heart was beating out of my chest, and I scattered to the side of the trail. It was the perfect case of false evidence appearing real . . . and I could have stopped, turned around, and decided that the risk of encountering an actual snake on that trail was just too high, but instead I kept going because finishing the hike felt more important than giving into my fear. If I had turned around, I would have missed the beautiful panoramic view at the top of the mountain. Life is just too short to miss those things. When we allow fear of the unknown to take the wheel, we head in the wrong direction, away from the things we most value, and simultaneously our world gets smaller. While our values may be different, and we all want different things, where we can all agree is that we want to live a life that feels freer and fuller. So, like me, and like Kate, and like so many others . . . when challenged with the anxiety and overwhelm that comes with things that are uncertain, we are invited to feel the fear and keep moving toward the unknown . . . because that's where the good stuff lives.

LET'S WORK TOWARD CHANGE . . .

My challenge to you is to think about your relationship with uncertainty. Think about how you tended to respond during the times when situations presented themselves that made you feel unsure around what the outcome would be. Maybe it was going off to college, or making a career change, or deciding to commit to something or someone, or deciding to have children, or waiting on that test result. Or maybe, on a smaller level, it's deciding which restaurant you should eat at, or what you should do for the holidays . . . the point is, we don't have to look very far (at all) for uncertainty—we are presented with the opportunity to resist it or welcome it all the time. Inviting uncertainty into our life is temporarily scary, but resisting it guarantees that we won't live a life as full as we hoped it would be.

Where do you fall on the spectrum of welcoming? Do you crave certainty? Do you love not knowing, but only when it comes to the fun stuff? A simple way to consider your relationship with anxiety is thinking about how you handled the 2020 pandemic . . . nobody did it "perfectly," but how difficult was all the uncertainty for you and how did it impact your well-being?

Consider what it might be like, how your feelings might change, or how your life might change if you opened up your arms just a bit wider to the unknown.

What is one thing you are willing to do today or tomorrow to welcome uncertainty? I.e., Take a different route to work, say "yes" to trying something new, or going on a solo one-day retreat . . . the possibilities (from big to small) are limitless. Meet yourself where you're at and keep it realistic!

RECLAIM

YOUR

LIFE

Chapter 7

YOU'RE INVITED INTO PRESENCE

"All negativity is caused by an accumulation of psychological time and denial of the present. Unease, anxiety, tension, stress, worry— all forms of fear—are caused by too much future, and not enough presence. Guilt, regret, resentment, grievances, sadness, bitterness, and all forms of nonforgiveness are caused by too much past, and not enough presence."
—ECKHART TOLLE

I can't tell you how often I have to remind myself to slow down my brain and body and invite myself to just be right there in that moment, where my feet are. Learning and practicing the art of being present is incredibly powerful. At the end of the chapter we will talk about the "how" when it comes to practicing presence, but first let's think about the "why" and consider the invitation in. I think it's true that suffering happens when we are either drifting back into the past or floating mindlessly into the possibilities of the future. The truth is, I'm no Eckhart Tolle, and for me (and maybe you too) practicing presence doesn't come easy. I admit that the knowledge of the topic of presence often far surpasses my ability to practice it. But what I hope you're hearing in this book is that it's not about getting it right 100 percent of the time—it's about moving toward wholehearted living and growth through a willingness to be a work in progress . . . or a bit of a hot mess.

What does it mean to practice presence and why is it so important for our mental and emotional health? Practicing presence means being only in the moment you are in—because, as you probably know all too well, you can be physically in one place and mentally time-traveling to another. That time-traveling, whether it's back to the past or toward the future, is the source of most all of our distress, negative feelings, despair, overwhelm, anxiety, and more. We have absolutely no power to change the past and very little control over what happens in the future. So let's pause for a minute here and think about how much time we spend trying to future forecast or walk back into the past to worry about things we can't fix. I bet the answer is . . . too damn much!

I'm not saying, "Don't think about the past or the future". . . I mean, it would be nice if we had the ability to move through the world Zen AF, but for most of us, in the modern world we live in, that's just not realistic. Thinking about the past and dreaming or planning for the future are just part of being human, and also an important part of understanding who we are, what really matters to us, and what direction we want to travel toward. We can learn from the past, but learning from the past is only helpful if we're willing to put that learning into practice—and we can only do that in the very moment we are living in. We can dream of, and plan for, the future—but since none of it is guaranteed to go as planned, we really have only the experience of right now. The bottom line is, when we overindulge in time-travel (going forward or back) we miss out on the right now moment . . . the place life is actually happening for us.

So why is it so hard for us to be present? There are a lot of reasons it's hard to be present—but things like the fast-paced world we live in, comparison, fear of judgment or loss, unresolved trauma, mental health issues like anxiety, depression, and ADHD seem to be the biggest contributing factors.

For the sake of not spending too much time telling you things that you already know: we have constant access to knowledge at out fingertips (literally). I mean, think about it . . . we pick up our phone and within the matter of ten seconds could be alerted about a mass shooting, a natural disaster, our kid's piano lesson that we forgot about, and what cute arts and crafts project our mom friend is doing with her kids while we're barely managing to keep our shit together. We are flooded with sensory input and information that our brains don't have the ability to organize and file all at once. When we get constantly pulled out of our own experience (which is really just our present moment) we start to adapt to that experience, and that flood of information becomes our norm—and even though we might know it's not "healthy," we are pulled by the need to "be in the know," or not miss anything because . . . FOMO! During the pandemic, I often had to remind my clients (and myself) to turn off the alerts on their phone, to shut off the news, and leave their device in their bedroom just so they could get a reprieve from the anxiety and sense of overwhelm caused by too much information and so little ability to make an impact—helplessness.

When it comes to unresolved trauma (bad shit that happened in the past that we don't know how to or never got the opportunity to deal with), being disconnected from the present moment, and even disassociating from the brain and body is a common experience. People who have experienced trauma learned that being "in the moment" wasn't safe (because for them, sadly, it truly wasn't), so they often float back or ahead in an attempt to experience less physical or emotional pain—it's how they learned to protect themselves and cope with really hard (sometimes unimaginable) things. Being in the present moment is a skill that needs to be learned—and for people with unresolved trauma, that means going back and getting the help they need to feel safe and supported in their present reality.

Anxiety ("the big A," as I call it), perfectionism, and the fear of being judged are also realities that mess with people's ability to be in the present moment. As I mentioned earlier in the book, we can really be anxious only when we're thinking about the past or future—so when people struggle with symptoms of anxiety it's usually because they're living everywhere but in the now. Anxiety is often created and maintained by the fear that if we don't do things "just right" or "perfectly" we will be discounted, left out, or poorly judged—it is incredibly difficult (almost impossible) to live well in the present moment when we are constantly planning for the next best move, or second-guessing the things we have done or said in the past.

Depression also puts up a big middle finger to presence because it makes us feel so stuck in whatever emotion we are experiencing that we don't want to exist in the present moment—there's too much pain there. Getting out of the present moment by sleeping, watching TV, or numbing out on food, drugs, or alcohol (not just for people who experience depression) is a way to try to escape the reality of the big and difficult emotions that live in the right now moment.

ADHD (a disorder you'll hear more about in my own story) is the queen bee when it comes to distraction and creating barriers for being able to stay in the present moment. Because of the different neurological wiring that people with ADHD have, they are inclined to try to take on a lot of tasks and projects, have five million thoughts in their brain at once, and therefore feel flustered, overwhelmed, and unable to be present because there's just TOO much going on.

The problem is, all this talk about presence can often make us women feel like we're just failing at one more thing—I don't want you to hear that here. Don't listen to the influencer who's storying about being present while on a walk with her perfectly dressed kids—I mean, she has clearly lost the plot on that one! I want you to hear that there's no use in shaming ourselves, or our loved ones, for not being perfectly present every moment because it's often something we are unaware of and don't choose—it's a struggle that is very real and relevant to the fast and complex world we live in.

MY INVITATION IN . . .

This is the part where I get to share my own story of struggle, in this case, with presence. And in case you haven't heard this already, just because I am a therapist and have the training and tools to help other people with their mental health, it (clearly) doesn't mean I'm immune to struggle. (You're probably thinking: "Yes, we know, Kaitlin, you're all kinds of hot mess.") I'm good with you recognizing that I'm a bit of a hot mess—because my hope is that through my own story and willingness to be vulnerable, you're willing to see the parts of yourself that have been hard to look at and the parts of yourself that need some more love and attention in order to evolve.

"The brain of a person with ADHD is like a fighter jet with a sensitive guidance system. No matter how hard the pilot tries to steer the fighter jet in the right direction, the guidance system does not respond in the same way that other jets might. Distractions overwhelm the typical functioning of the ADHD fighter jet. The communications system picks

Mindfulness is about the ability to be exactly where your feet are . . . experiencing the feelings and sensations that are showing up for you in that particular moment in time.

up multiple stations and conversations at once, making it difficult to sort through incoming messages. The ADHD fighter jet's brakes are loose, allowing the pilot's thoughts to be whisked miles away and making course correction difficult." When this quote, from a blog sent to me by my own provider, came into my in-box I felt . . . stunned. Why stunned? Because I felt like it was the perfect description of my brain and what I experience on the daily.

Let me back up a bit. Even though I always thought I might have ADHD, I didn't take it upon myself to reach out for professional help, or an official diagnosis (yes, you're noticing a theme here), until mid-pandemic, when it felt like the wheels were falling off, so to speak.

I am somebody who loves to be busy, has a high capacity to work on multiple things, and has always been passionate about many things, so when I tried to explain the intensity of my feelings of overwhelm, or the disorganization I experience, it often gets brushed off by me (and others) as a sign that I need to slow down. "You're just trying to do too much," they say. It's true sometimes. And I've gotten to the point where I can recognize that I need to slow it on down—mom life is challenging and then you add the layers, and it can feel impossible to keep up. But the type of struggle and inability to stay present and on track that I experience started to feel far from normal, and I knew something was different. In talking with a psychiatrist who specializes in adult ADHD diagnosis, I learned that it's not normal to lose track of so much on the daily and to suffer because of it. When I reflect back on my years of life thus far, I can see that things like lost keys, misplaced checks, forgotten payments, and all kinds of other mishaps have been a part of my life WELL before having kids to blame those things on.

The reason my ADHD was missed is because, to me, it didn't look like what I thought it should—as a child I did well in school (minus math), I went to college, got a graduate degree, have had great jobs, and am successful in my career. I couldn't reckon with my ability to listen so effectively to my clients (I mean, it's kind of an important part of being a therapist) and also have a disorder that involved struggle paying attention. Later I learned that in the ADHD world, this skill is called hyperfocus, the ability to pay close attention to the things you're most interested in or fascinated by. ADHD comes with many strengths, and for my career, hyperfocus is a gift—until I look up from my desk and my twenty-minute writing project has turned into an hour and I've left no time for myself to regroup before the next task at hand.

I believe it was the pandemic (let's just agree to blame everything shitty on that) and a particular event (which I'll share more about in a minute) that pushed me over the edge into recognizing I was deep in ADHD struggle. During the heart of the pandemic, the year 2020, like so many women, I was trying to run a home, work on creative projects, and juggle childcare and educational needs, as well as running a business and writing a book, all while trying to make sure everyone was happy (ish). The weight of all that increased my struggle with things like my ability to start and finish a task, remember things, keep track of schedules, and DEFINTELY with my ability to be in the present moment. What I didn't consider about ADHD, but understood about mental health in general, is that it can ebb and flow throughout the seasons of your life. Meaning that in different seasons, and due to different life circumstances, your struggle can get bigger or smaller . . . and even (seemingly) disappear. So as it turns out, beyond triggering my anxiety, that global pandemic was also an invitation for my ADHD to come and party.

There was one particular day, after thirty-seven years of living with this scattered sense of reality, that I decided I needed to take control of my narrative when it came to my ability to be more mindful and present. My husband had asked me to take his necklace to the jeweler to get fixed . . . and prefaced it with, "Please don't lose it." Well, that necklace, given to him by his parents when he first became a firefighter years ago, ended up sitting in my car for weeks before I eventually lost it—worst wife award over here! I put it in my purse with the intention of bringing it to the jeweler, but instead I must have thrown it away during one of my frantic "ew, my purse is so gross and full of trash" moments. The day came where I had to face the music and tell him that I had lost his "good luck charm," and he was (rightfully) disappointed about the loss of something that held such meaning. That SAME day I lost the office keys, and I remember my usually very patient husband looking at me with a look of frustration (and maybe even disgust) and saying he needed some space. Don't worry, not space like the leaving me kind—but he needed to go for a walk to deal with his feelings around my inability to keep things straight (which he would never verbalize, but being the empath I am, I knew it). That moment felt like rock bottom for me when it came to my inability to be present and keep track of things.

So what am I doing to be more intentional about being present? Most importantly, I've realized that I have to really lower the bar when it comes to the expectations I put on myself to take on the world and keep it all straight—because my brain doesn't work like everyone else's. Being present is something I have to practice, in small ways, every day or else I become (even more) of a hot mess, miss out on important moments with loved ones, and let myself down. I am undecided on how I will move forward with the treatment of my ADHD, but for now I am starting with taking on less, doing lots of grounding, getting extra help with organization and, in general, focusing on things that help quiet the noise and invite me to be present in my beautiful and messy day-to-day.

YOUR INVITATION IN . . .

As you know by now, you don't need ADHD to struggle with presence, you just need to be an imperfect human being like everyone else on the face of this planet. While you may not be QUITE as big of a hot mess as me when it comes to the topic of presence—from a psychology perspective we know that everyone struggles with their ability to be present from time to time. We also know how incredibly healing and powerful it can be for people, including you and me, to learn what we call "mindfulness" skills in order to decrease negative emotion (depression, worry, anxiety, fear, etc.) and increase our ability to accept, and even welcome, our life as it is.

When I use mindfulness skills in my work with clients, it's not necessarily about increasing their positive emotion—but instead increasing their ability to recognize that if they come back to present moment, they are, in fact (in that moment), alive and well. So what is mindfulness anyway? You probably hear that term often, it's thrown around like a dang beach ball on the Internet, but it's not always represented accurately. Mindfulness isn't something achieved for just three minutes a day while you're meditating (p.s., remember that three minutes is a long time for somebody with ADHD brain). It's about the ability to be exactly where your feet are . . . experiencing the feelings and sensations that are showing up for you in that particular moment in time.

So many of my clients have struggled with debilitating anxiety, the type that makes them not show up for important things, cancel at the last minute, and even not leave their house for days on end. Their anxiety, like all of ours, lives and breathes on the things that "could" or "might" happen in the future. My job is to help my clients cut off air to their anxiety, to give it no more fuel to thrive on. The best way I (and research) know to do that is to teach the mindfulness skills necessary for them to STAY in the present moment.

When my client Bailey came to see me, she was feeling guilt and shame around what she described as her difficulty being "present" with her children. I mean . . . let's be real, sometimes they're not fun to be present with. But in all seriousness, Bailey was recognizing, as we do sometimes, that the way she was actually living out her life as "mom" didn't match the kind of mom she wanted to be. It's a really painful thing to recognize we are living out of alignment with our values, but not as painful as paying the price for staying out of line with them. So, after doing some major normalizing of the facts that this mom shit is really hard, I helped Bailey recognize that a big reason she was struggling to be present was because she was dealing with a lot of anxiety. She had struggled with anxiety before, but always felt she could manage it, until kids and the pandemic made her a stay-at-home working mom (that's a thing now), teacher, booty wiper, tear dryer, and everything else in between.

The way she had learned to cope with her anxiety over the years (regardless of what it was centered around) was to overthink, overprepare, and please everyone else (except for herself) so she couldn't be judged or criticized. Anxiety lied to her (as it does) and told her, "Everything will be OK so long as you're prepared, productive, and always ready." The problem with anxiety's lie is that it causes us to crash and burn, and to lose sight of the stuff that we care about the most. Bailey and I worked on addressing her lifelong anxiety by examining the beliefs that kept it going, facing her fears head-on, and learning the mindfulness skills (I'll explain a few of my personal favorites in a minute) needed to pull her brain and body back to the present moment.

LET'S WORK TOWARD CHANGE . . .

It's not an easy task to quiet the constant noise that is modern life, nor is it practical to think we're going to "nail" it when it comes to being present with our children, partners, friends, family, or work. The goal is to get to a place where, just like with every other invitation we've explored in this book, you are more often able and empowered to take the wheel and steer yourself in the direction you hope to go (toward your values).

Here are a few simple things you can do to practice presence: 1. Notice and catch yourself when you're time-traveling. 2. Get grounded. 3. Add a daily (ish) meditation practice to your routine. 4. Play. We can't make change unless we notice that we are engaging in a pattern, so the most important thing we can do is call ourselves on our own bullshit—give yourself a prompt like, "I'm time-traveling again . . . let's come back to this moment." The second thing on this list is a simple grounding exercise.

As you know, I'm ALL about keeping it simple and "doable" when it comes to mental health practices. So, when it comes to grounding, you don't have to do anything Oprah-worthy here, other than feel your feet touching the floor, look around you and notice what you see, smell, or taste. The grounding exercise I just shared is a simple way to invite your brain to get back into the prefrontal cortex (where it can think straight) and your body to come back into the present moment. That simple exercise is something you can do over and over, on the daily, and will greatly improve your ability to show up for your right now life.

Implementing a daily meditation practice will support your ability to sit with whatever thoughts and feelings show up for you, without trying to get rid of them, fix them, or solve them—all of which pull us out of the present. I say daily (ish) because, as you know by now, I'm not a big fan of setting standards for ourselves that are hard to meet and then make us feel like we're dropping the ball. Grace. Lots of grace.

Lastly, try to play . . . have you ever noticed how present your children are when they are playing? I sometimes am so envious of my own children's ability to just be content exactly where they are—we could all use more of that in our life. Here's the good news—we can play too . . . and I don't mean you have to play Barbies, or build Legos (though you can if that's your thing), but find something to engage in like hiking, playing cards, traveling, adventuring, or anything that allows you to just be right where you are.

How do you think practicing presence might improve your life in one (or all) of these realms: self-care, parenting, your relationships, your career/work life, your creativity, your ability to give to your community?

What is one (small) thing you can commit to doing each day to work on being more present (for me, it's just a few minutes of breath work or meditation while the coffee is brewing)?

What will your "mantra" be around presence; in other words, what can you tell yourself to bring yourself back into the moment? Mine is, "Be where your feet are." You can use mine . . . or create your own!

The Practice

Chapter 8

YOU'RE INVITED TO HOLD SPACE FOR MULTIPLE TRUTHS

"You're allowed to be both a masterpiece and a work in progress simultaneously."

—SOPHIA BUSH

I'm going to ask you to do something right out of the gate in this chapter—pay attention to how often you see the words "both and." OK, let's resume.

Rigid or black-and-white thinking is one of the most universal and common contributing factors to our own experience of suffering. What I mean is, when we are made to believe there is only one "right" way to do things like parent, love, or lead we limit ourselves and move through the world in ways that keeps us stuck and disconnected from reality. In the fields of psychology and neuroscience, it is widely believed that flexible thinking is a skill that is critical for humans to experience mental and emotional wellness and resiliency. In my clinical work, if I had to pick the most common factor that plays into my clients' sense of unhappiness or pain—it would undoubtedly be rigid ways of thinking that then lead to unhealthy behavioral patterns. The belief that is often endorsed is that people (including us) and experiences are either "all good or all bad." This type of all-or-nothing thinking is sticky and unforgiving, and doesn't allow us, or others, the space to evolve throughout the many different seasons of our life.

While it might feel safer to draw clean lines of "either or" around things—the reality is that life is pretty complex AND so is being human. Nature is one of the greatest teachers when it comes to showing us what it looks like to hold multiple truths. We would never classify the ocean as only tumultuous and chaotic, because we know that it can sometimes be quiet and serene too. When we learn to leave more space for gray, and for multiple things to be true at the same time, we give ourselves and our loved ones the gift of grace and a life that is freer and, undoubtedly, fuller.

Why do we engage in rigid thinking anyway? Let's take a brief dive into why in the heck we engage with this kind of thinking if it ultimately makes us feel crappy and suffer. First, it's important to point out that some people struggle with mental health or personality disorders in which rigid thinking is a symptom, and so it's harder (not impossible) for them to change. But for most of us, our rigid thinking is a product of *BOTH* nature *and* nurture. So here we are, already in the first section of this chapter, recognizing one of the many "both ands" of life. By nature, some of us are biologically and neurologically wired to think in ways that leave less room for gray. By nurture (the way we are raised to understand and experience life), many of us were exposed to rigid and limited thinking and learned that was the safest, maybe even only, way to exist in the world. Whether it's due to nature, nurture, or both—rigid thinkers seek experiences that reinforce their belief that life is safest seen through the lens of "either or" and "black or white." Of course, there is a spectrum of rigid thinking, where some of us engage in it more than others, but on some level most of us get stuck from time to time in the seductive web of wanting just one thing to be true—because, let's face it, it's simpler and less anxiety-provoking. We want firm soil, but we're given shifting sands.

Just beneath the surface of our rigid (unhelpful) thinking live our old frenemies—perfectionism and fear. Opening up our minds to accepting multiple truths in life is both freeing and scary. We'll get to the freeing part in a little bit, but let's talk about the part where we feel scared AF to accept some of the following truths about life: it's both beautiful and painful, it's colorful and dark, there's birth and there's death, there's love and there's loss, there's everything and there's nothing, there's less and there's more, you'll laugh and you'll cry, you'll win and you'll lose, you'll suffer and you'll rejoice, you'll fall and you'll get back up. There is just no escaping the *both ands* of life.

As we talked about in earlier chapters, perfectionism and fear tell us the lie that we need to engage in overcontrol (doing way too much and being way too extra) in order to be safe and happy. In order to engage in overcontrol (something I don't suggest) you would need to reject the idea of multiple truths because it makes things too difficult to predict and therefore control. Enter the power struggle that exists when we spend way too much time trying to live in the land of certainty and a one-dimensional world that doesn't actually exist.

We can find so much more space and freedom in life when we leave room for multiple truths. The reality is, no matter what our anxious or primitive brain wants us to believe, things can't be reduced to all good or all bad, all black or all white, all positive or all negative. Once we learn to welcome that truth, we are able to live more freely and fully. When we don't leave room for the gray parts of life, we don't make space for the variety of experiences and emotions that life has to offer us. In other words, we can't live wholeheartedly when we resist the idea that the world is a complex place; where often the only truth is that there isn't just one truth. The acceptance of the complex nature of life and the reality of multiple truths depends on our ability to engage in flexible thinking. Flexible thinking is a learned skill . . . sure, some of us are born with the ability to learn it better or raised in an environment where it's more strongly encouraged, but nonetheless, it is a skill that needs to be learned and practiced. We will dive into the "how" behind working on increasing mental flexibility, but first let me share my experience with leaning into the idea of multiple truths.

MY INVITATION IN . . .

For me, living in the world of "both and" means having the courage to accept that life is many things all at once. When it comes to parenting, it is both hard AND beautiful. Parenting seems to be the ultimate invitation to embracing life's multiple truths and, if we take it, into practicing mental flexibility. When we start off our journey as moms we all have ideas, based on what we've seen or been told, about what it will be like to be a mother . . . and let's just be honest, most of those ideas turn out to be total bullshit. Just about the only thing we get right when it comes to our imaginary experience of having kids is that we'll love them more than anything in the world . . . and even then, we couldn't fathom what that would actually feel like until we were living and breathing that experience. There's no doubt that having children does so many things to us, but one of the things it does *for us* is wake us up and call for us to deal with our emotional baggage (or shit) so that we can parent and love well.

I don't think you'll be surprised to hear this by now, since I've laid so much of my story on the table (totally going against the whole outdated notion that therapists should be a blank slate), but I am a bit of a perfectionist in disguise— even though I can be a hot mess from time to time, I like it when things are clear and certain. You know what's not clear and certain? Anything when it comes to children and parenthood. Whenever I think I understand something or have finally figured out a pattern when it comes to my kids' sleep, behavior, or emotional well-being . . . life just sort of laughs in my face, as if to say, "I'll show you!" Case in point . . . we sleep trained the hell out of my first child, Mia. At twelve weeks old, Mia slept through the night and we felt like we totally NAILED it when it came to sleep training . . . like seriously, what are all these parents complaining about anyway? Don't they know that a few nights of crying are well worth creating a child who can self-soothe and get consistent and restful sleep? "We're just so natural at this," I thought . . . well, we had it coming. I bet you can guess what I'm going to say next, but we tried all the same sleep techniques with our second and third children and it didn't work. Alex and Jack had different needs when it came to comfort than Mia did—and in order to meet their needs, I needed to let go of my rigid thinking tied to what I believed to be true about their needs so I could actually see what it was they required. One ended up needing acid reflux medicine and diet changes, and the other ended up needing ear tubes, and they both just needed us to be flexible and patient. Do you see how rigid thinking, especially when it comes to parenting, can keep us stuck from moving forward in a way that's intuitive?

While the sleep example seems sort of trivial in the big scheme of things (although every mom on earth has obsessed over their children's sleep at one point or another), it is just one example of how we are invited, often in subtle ways, to embrace the both ands of life and practice mental flexibility. The biggest "why" behind my stepping into the idea of accepting multiple truths is both because I want to live more freely AND I want my children to as well. As Virginia Satir, famous author and therapist, once said: "Feelings of worth can flourish only in an atmosphere where individual differences are appreciated, mistakes are tolerated, communication is open, and rules are flexible—the kind of atmosphere that is found in a nurturing family." I want my children to know that I see them, and that I honor the complexity of their experience and the complexity of life in general—the idea they can be so many things, and already are, all at once.

Here are some "both ands," or multiple truths, that I am learning to hold—maybe they'll resonate with you too: I can be a good mom AND an ambitious mom. I can love them AND create boundaries. I can be the one who helps AND the one who receives help. I can be uncertain AND invigorated. I can be exhausted AND grateful. I can be anxious AND willing to take a step forward. I can love my parents AND decide to do things differently. I can be a good friend, mom, or partner AND evolve. I can be fearful AND brave. I can love them AND want more. I can play it safe AND be willing to take a worthy risk. I can be a woman AND demand that I get my own needs met. I can be in pain AND grow. I can experience loss AND peace in the same day. I can experience mom guilt AND know, at my core, it's important that I say go. I can say no (or yes) to Elf on the Shelf AND my kids will experience the holidays all the same. I can no longer fit into my pre-pandemic or pre-baby jeans AND still be beautiful. I can be a granola mom AND then decide to serve cheap frozen pizza for the hell of it. I can care about exercise AND take the time to listen to my body and rest. I can feel like an imposter sometimes AND know that I'm worthy. I can . . . AND . . . You can . . . AND . . . We can . . . AND.

You're likely getting the drift by now, but in order to create more healthy and flexible thinking, we have to be willing to break the rules (or those unhelpful/shitty beliefs) that we've bought into along the way around the idea that things are "either or" and "black or white." Earlier, I wrote that life can be both beautiful and painful . . . and we all know that to be true, on a logical level, but the experience of pain can make us so terrified that we, ironically, don't allow ourselves to feel joy. We've all heard, or said, "I'm just waiting for the other shoe to drop." Let's talk about that sentiment for a minute—the idea that when something is going well, or something happened the way we hoped it would, we should only *minimally* enjoy it because either it won't last long or because eventually it will end and we will be hurt. There is so much wrong with that logic, and I admit I've endorsed it myself in the past, but the truth is, yes, the pain will come (suffering is an inevitable part of life) AND it won't hurt any less because we were waiting for it to happen. Perhaps the human experience seems less vulnerable for people when they don't fully allow themselves to experience the depths of joy, but the truth is, not experiencing the depths of joy doesn't keep us from feeling the depths of pain. If we can accept that life is both beautiful AND painful, we make more space for joy and gratitude and less space for fear.

Let's not live our lives "waiting for the other shoe to drop." I see this sentiment play out quite often in my one-on-one work, especially with women. For a multitude of reasons and complex truths about society and culture, I think we women are more conditioned to keep our feet on the ground, so to speak, and to expect less. It's not always the case that women feel this way (I mean, we are in a chapter about multiple truths and all), but it does seem to trend true that, in comparison to men, women feel immensely more responsibility for the well-being of those around them. While we've come a long way when it comes to opportunities for women to be more than just caretakers, caretaking is still often seen as our primary role and we feel the pressure to keep it all together and be prepared in case things fall apart. When the possibility of disaster is always just beneath the surface, we spend a lot of time overpreparing, worrying, and planning—which are, let's be real, total joy inhibitors.

While we likely won't wake up suddenly with less responsibility to care for our loved ones, nor would we want to, we CAN decide to more fully step into the land of multiple truths—the land that allows us to recognize that our life will be both beautiful AND painful no matter how much we prepare. And in recognizing that "waiting for the other shoe to drop" won't actually help us or the ones we love feel less pain, maybe we could stop denying ourselves feelings of gratitude and joy . . . we deserve those feelings, we've earned them.

The learning to accept, and live into the truth, that life is both beautiful AND painful is what therapeutic or self-growth work is really all about. When people come to see a therapist like me, it's often because they are in pain and unable to find their way out of suffering—they want to grow, change, or heal, but they don't have the resources or the vision to see their starting point. Like life, the work of healing and change isn't linear—it's up, down, and around. Healing is both beautiful AND painful.

I've worked with so many brave souls who are doing the work of healing from trauma, and I'm in my own process of cleaning out old wounds too. Yes, your therapist is likely in therapy (in fact, it's ethically prudent that therapists do their own work) . . . we can have the "tools" AND still find ourselves needing another's expertise. Especially when it comes to trauma healing, I know that we can't do effective work until we start to recognize and accept our experiences of "both, and." The truth of it is, even the people who hurt us the worst weren't ALL bad ALL the time—and part of the healing process is accepting the truth that we can have a wide spectrum of memories and feelings when it comes to our most traumatic experiences. Trauma work calls us to move from rigid thinking, the kind of thinking that was meant to keep us safe, to more flexible thinking so that we can see what happened for the complex experience it likely was.

Many faces come to mind when I think of what the work of acceptance of multiple truths looks like in practice—but there is one woman whose experience never escapes me. Georgia, a seventy-year-old woman, came to me for help around dealing with her feelings of anxiety and depression after living through the massive Northern California wildfires of 2017 and the repeated fires that have threatened her home every year since. Georgia and her husband had worked hard throughout their life and were proud of the beautiful wine-country property where they raised their sons. When she spoke of the property as it was before the fires, you could feel her deep and spiritual connection with the nature and environment of her home. She tended to the land, hiked for hours a day, gardened, cooked, and felt she was exactly where she needed to be. While they didn't lose their home in the fire, their property and everything around them burned down. The beautiful oaks that were hundreds of years old were suddenly gone, cars and possessions were burned, and the landscape was completely changed. But as we worked through the whole of her experience, we recognized that the real loss had nothing to do with things and everything to do with the loss of her sense of security and safety. She felt disoriented in a world that looked and felt so different—the other shoe dropped; it had all been too good to be true.

We talked about the fact that even if she had known it was going to happen it wouldn't have made it any less painful. Once she accepted that healing would mean she would have to be willing to walk through the painful memories and the beautiful ones, she was able to hold space for the idea that she, herself, could experience both pain and joy at the same time. She started going on walks again, planting seeds for oak trees that she (laughingly) declared she would be long gone before they grew past the height of a toddler. Georgia taught me so much more about healing, and life really, than I could have ever taught her—and maybe it's because she had so much life experience, but I have never seen someone engage in flexible thinking so quickly and create so much space for life's pain AND beauty. Experiences like this with my clients are incredibly healing. They heal me AND I heal them . . . both things are true. And isn't that just the beauty of real connection? We get lifted by lifting each other.

LET'S WORK TOWARD CHANGE . . .

So now that you've learned the "why" behind accepting multiple truths and increasing mental flexibility (aka flexible thinking), maybe you're wondering how it applies to you, or where you can get started doing this work in a practical way.

I've got you covered. A great place to start is to think about places and spaces in your life where you sometimes feel stuck or experience rigid thinking. For me this kind of thinking historically comes up when it comes to parenting, but maybe it's somewhere different for you. Maybe you're in the camp of "waiting for the other shoe to drop," and never fully allowing yourself to play, dream, or discover because you're too afraid of the pain or disappointment that could come. Spoiler alert—pain is coming, but if you allow room for it, joy can come along for the ride. Maybe you believe that if you've been one thing, you can't be another. Or maybe you get stuck in perfectionistic "all or nothing" thinking—that lie that tells you you're either always the best or always the worst.

Wherever you are on the spectrum of accepting multiple truths, we can all benefit from more often leaning into the idea that many things are true at once. When it comes to practicing and living into this concept, it starts with recognizing the many "both ands" in your own life and noticing how it feels when you acknowledge their coexistence. Another way you can play with this concept is by noticing how often you hear yourself and the people in your life engaging in rigid thinking and ask yourself this one question: "But also, what else is true?"

Do you tend to be a rigid thinker or do you make space for multiple truths? Maybe you were once less rigid, or more rigid . . . if that's true, reflect on why. I.e., When I was a new mom, I was WAY more rigid than I am now.

What multiple truths do you have the hardest time accepting in your life, or in the world around you? I.e., That we can both love our kids and want/need time away from them.

What would it look like if you lifted the weight of rigid thinking off your shoulders? What would there be more room for in your life if you, for example, accepted the fact that there are good parts and hard parts to almost everything in life?

The Practice

Chapter 9

YOU'RE INVITED TO CHANGE YOUR MIND-SET

"If parents want to give their children a gift, the best thing they can do is to teach their children to love challenges, be intrigued by mistakes, enjoy effort, and keep on learning. That way, their children don't have to be slaves of praise. They will have a lifelong way to build and repair their own confidence."

—CAROL S. DWECK

Our mind-set informs the way we move through our own life, including our parenting, our relationships, and our career. Mind-set affects how we love and lead ourselves and others. You may remember from the beginning of the book, but my "why" behind writing to you here is to find a better way forward both for us (you and me) and for them (our children). I believe women deserve a more authentic and graceful way into personal growth AND when we're committed to the process of (imperfect) evolution it will change the trajectory of our children's lives for the better.

You've heard the saying before, but it rings so true, that when a plane's cabin pressure drops we MUST put on our own oxygen mask before we can put one on our loved ones'. The mind-set we choose to endorse and live by arguably leaves a bigger impact on our children, and all those around us for that matter, than anything else we do as parents. I'll dive a bit deeper into what a "growth mind-set" is in a minute, but it's important to know that it's really unlikely that our children will develop a healthy mind-set if we don't have one ourselves. No shame, no blame, just a choice to move forward a bit more informed and willing to change.

In this chapter, I'm going to walk us through the concepts of "growth versus fixed mind-sets," and then discuss how we can work toward cultivating a healthier way forward. Our mind-set is ultimately responsible for our perspective—the lens through which we see the whole picture of life. Sometimes we need to be able to zoom out, to take a wide-angle view of life, so that we can see things like truth, hope, and a way forward. Sometimes we need to zoom in, so that we can face what's right in front of us in that very moment. The practice of being flexible, to both zoom in and zoom out and adjust our actions accordingly, is what allows us to maintain a healthy mind-set—one that allows for growth.

But first, let's consider why we should ditch and reject toxic positivity. Cultivating a growth mind-set is not the same as being positive at all costs—and probably like you, I reject the type of toxic positivity found way too easily in today's social media/self-help world, where the answers seem to always (and inappropriately) be "just be positive" or "positive vibes only!" F. that. You know why? It's total BS. Life is not all rainbows and unicorns, not everything happens for a reason, and a strong dose of positivity doesn't solve every problem. Sure, there is always the opportunity for us to grow from the myriad challenges life throws our way, but we can't actually grow if we don't first feel our REAL feelings about a tough situation . . . and our real feelings are often uncomfortable and negative. And that's OK . . . that's REAL, that's HUMAN.

Toxic positivity (as defined by me) is the rejection of any emotion that is seen as negative or inherently "bad," and the compulsive pushing toward happiness and positivity, even when it's not authentic . . . it's downright wishful thinking. This type of positivity-at-all-cost attitude may have been born out of good intentions, but it represents a gross and dangerous misinterpretation of people's emotional and psychological experience. Toxic positivity LACKS perspective, honesty, and the honoring of the human experience that includes a wide spectrum of shitty, wonderful, and in-between feelings.

One of the big downsides of being influenced by toxic positivity is that it often causes people an even harder time holding compassion for themselves (like we as women need any more help with that) and makes it hard to see the very real issues they are facing and how they might be able to cope/problem-solve.

At its core, toxic positivity is the denial and avoidance of uncomfortable feelings, and as we've learned, avoidance ends up only making us feel worse and can increase our already unwanted feelings of anxiety and depression. Let's do an experiment really quick. . . . I want you to try NOT to think about a pink elephant. What popped into your head right away? The damn pink elephant, right? That's my point. We can't effectively avoid our real thoughts and feelings by pushing them away or labeling them as something they're not.

So let's just agree that next time you see #positivibesonly or #positivityistheanswer or #alwayspositive underneath a social media post, you'll scroll on. Please, don't make life harder than it already is by placing judgment on yourself for feeling anything other than EXACTLY how you feel. You'll just be adding another layer of shit onto a shit sandwich.

So, what is a growth mind-set anyway? The concept of a "growth mind-set" has been talked about a lot in recent literature, and especially in the field of education. A Stanford professor and author of the book *Mindset*, Carol Dweck, first defined the concepts of "growth and fixed mind-sets."

One of the major findings from her extensive and impactful research was that a "growth mind-set," versus a "fixed mind-set," leads to children being more successful and resilient. The big takeaway for parents, teachers, and mentors? When we praise and encourage our children for working hard, putting in the effort, and doing hard things, they are much more likely to take on challenges in the future and continue to grow and improve—we create lifelong learners. But don't worry, when I say lifelong learners I don't mean they'll be in school for life, but that they'll be willing to find out what they need to know, and what they need to do, in order to adapt to life's changing tides. But when we hyperfocus on achievement and accolades (grades, awards, status) we tie our children to the belief that in order to be successful they have to be the "best" or "win," which discourages them from taking a chance and risking failure. Perfectionism (not the cute kind, but the damaging kind) and a fixed mind-set go hand in hand.

The ability to cultivate a growth mind-set is essential to our mental and emotional health because without it we tend to go in one of two ways: the land of rainbows and unicorns (toxic positivity) or the land of stuck and same (clearly two not-so-fancy terms I just made up). While I suppose it sounds nice to live in the land of rainbows and unicorns (toxic positivity) where everything "happens for a reason" and everything is perfect so long as you will it to be—it's both impossible to sustain and, as we know, damaging to ourselves and our loved ones. Living in the land of stuck and same might seem to promise safety, or that we won't get let down when life is inevitably hard and we struggle, but it also means we make little space for learning, opportunity, and sometimes even joy.

The way I see it, a growth mind-set (which I'll often refer to as a flexible mind-set) requires us to be able to hold multiple truths, tolerate uncertainty, and take calculated risks so that we can view life through an accurate and hopeful lens. When we are engaged with our growth mind-set, we recognize that it benefits us to try new things and seek opportunities to learn because it allows us to level up. The idea of "failing forward" resonates with me—the notion that when we fail, sure it's hard, but it also provides us with the opportunity to grow and go forward even better than before. When we cultivate a growth mind-set, we can see that even making mistakes or "failing" (a word we all dislike) can lead to learning, growth, change, and opportunity.

Let's talk about the fixed mind-set . . . and I'm just going to be honest here, while you're reading these paragraphs you're going to immediately think of somebody in your life who you're SURE has a fixed mind-set—it will be your mom, one of your children, your father in-law, your sister, or even your own dang self, and that's OK. It can be really hard to coexist and understand the motivation of our loved ones who live from a fixed mind-set . . . but let's consider that it's likely harder for them to move through the world in such a limiting way than it is for us to have to deal with them being consistently negative or "stuck." I guess what I'm saying is, let's practice holding both empathy and hope for ourselves or for the people in our lives who struggle to find flexibility in their mind-set because it's likely not their fault (remember the whole nature versus nurture convo?) AND it's not your job to change their perspective or feed into it either. Don't worry, we'll talk boundaries in the next chapter!

Somebody who has a fixed mind-set believes that when they "fail," they fail backward. Everything hangs on the outcome, so it feels safer to avoid challenges and/or give up before they even start. The painful part of living with a fixed mind-set is believing that you are born with certain characteristics or qualities and then you're stuck with those, and there's no way to move the needle. In more subtle ways, you can hear a fixed mind-set when people say things like, "Creativity isn't my thing" or "I'm not good at (insert anything here)." A growth mind-set might sound like, "When I did that before I wasn't so great at it, but I'm willing to try it again, and if I make a fool of myself . . . oh well, at least I've learned something new/had a new experience."

There are a few important takeaways before we move forward with my story/invitation in and then the "how to" when it comes to cultivating a stronger growth mind-set. We can help our children develop a growth mind-set, but only if we first develop ours. Adversity is an inevitable part of life and people with both fixed and growth mind-sets are faced with struggle. When the fixed mind-set is faced with challenge and they don't meet that challenge perfectly, they see only failure; whereas when the growth mind-set is faced with challenge they can hold both that it will be hard and that there'll be opportunity for growth. And lastly, we can ebb and flow (and of course grow) between the two mind-sets (especially when we're practicing the new skill of cultivating a growth mind-set).

MY INVITATION IN . . .

Not to pat myself on the back or anything, but I find myself leaning in to a flexible and growth mind-set more often than not—generally, I'm willing to find opportunity for growth in new experiences and take chances even when it feels emotionally painful. The culprit? Nature AND nurture. I think some of us are just born with personalities that lend themselves to either flexible or more rigid mind-sets—and I was born with the latter. We could go a layer deeper and imagine that me being the youngest of three, with fewer expectations (let's be real . . . you know parents are exhausted by the third), played into it as well. We tend to think a lot about all the ways our parents messed us up (and that's legit), but now that we're parents ourselves, I think it's important to consider the full picture. In other words, what are the areas where our parents fell short and what are the areas they did well in? Taking that into consideration helps us see what things felt supportive to the younger version of ourselves and what things didn't . . . from that reflection we can gain insight into what hand-me-down parenting we want to ditch and what we want to keep. My parents encouraged me as a child to try new things, and they normalized setbacks and mistakes as a natural part of life and growth. I wasn't made to feel "bad" or "dumb" when I couldn't do something—but instead encouraged to keep trying and/or make some adjustments. They helped me to cultivate a growth mind-set—and I am grateful for that and the opportunity and grit it's afforded me. Parents play a significant role in the type of mind-set their kids will adopt and live into and so do the other adults and mentors in children's lives. This is yet again another reason for us to work on cultivating a growth mind-set—so that we give our children the opportunity to do the same!

What I know now is that the only way my parents could have effectively taught me to keep my mind and heart open to "failing forward" is because they were willing to do so in their own life. Side note—I'm pretty confident that they doubted their parenting approach when they saw the amount of falling on my face that happened in my twenties, but while the learning curve was steep, I had a diverse range of experiences and came out alive, stronger, and (mostly) better for those experiences.

While I've never been an extreme risk-taker (traveling with abandon, skydiving, living without an agenda, etc.), I will say that I have taken some leaps, some that could be considered failures and some that could be considered successes. I can say, without doubt, that every challenge I've taken on has taught me something even when things didn't work out the way I thought they would. I don't think I always saw the opportunity for growth at the time I was taking on a new challenge or learning, but in retrospect, I can see that regardless of the outcome almost every experience is worthwhile.

When I was in my twenties, one of my big leaps was deciding to jump on a plane to Italy to work for an extended period of time as a production assistant . . . a job I wanted SO badly that I was relentlessly persistent about going after. The persistence paid off and I got the job. Once I was there, I often felt "out of my league" (because I was) as a twenty-two-year-old female among mostly all males in their thirties and forties with established jobs in media. During that time, my job mostly consisted of shoveling snow (real glamorous) so the big shots wouldn't slip when they walked out of the production truck, fetching coffee, driving the talent around in a way too small car on a way too small road, and gathering stats on cross-country skiers I had never heard of before . . . because, cross country-skiing? Anyway. I was around some BIG personalities who seemed hell-bent on making me recognize how insignificant I was in their world, and while it stung, I tried to turn my attention to the few higher-ups who led with grace and conviction. The hot

Sometimes we need to take the wide-lens view of life, so we can see the whole picture. . . . Other times we need to zoom in and see what's right in front of us. Wellness is the ability to do both.

Italian men, late nights of dancing, and lots of wine helped too . . . I mean, that's the stuff of dreams at twenty-two! There was a steep learning curve when it came to figuring out how to both work and play well, and I definitely burned the candle at both ends, and often made mistakes . . . but I don't think I can point to a single experience in my life that taught me more about breaking out of my comfort zone and taking a chance on myself.

Even though my role was small in the big scheme of the Olympics, the experience of working on such a large production at a young age taught me that if there was something I wanted in my life or my career I could go toward it—and even if I wasn't great at it right away, I would find a way to get better or jump ship if it wasn't for me.

So how is that whole growth mind-set thing going for me now? Well, I come up with and execute on ideas to help people prioritize their mental health (some of those ideas work, some don't), I put my name in the hat for speaking engagements as an expert (even if I'm not sure I'm expert enough), and I decided to write a book, even though I've never written one before and I technically don't have the time to. I do all of this because I am not afraid of failure. I've failed many times, and I've gotten up just as many. Do I like messing up? Hell no. Do I sometimes get stubborn and defensive . . . absolutely. But that stuff is just human nature; the "work" is in making sure we don't stop at stubbornness or defensiveness . . . that we go one step further and see what could be on the other side of the difficult experience.

I've learned that in my realm of career, entrepreneurship, and ESPECIALLY parenthood mistakes and missteps are certain—what matters is how we decide to cope with them and how we decide to move forward from there.

Here's the deal: you can't be perfectionistic and have a growth mind-set at the same time—the two things just don't go together. This doesn't mean you're disqualified if you're perfectionistic (I've already talked about my own struggle with perfectionism in certain realms of life), it just means you've got some work to do. In order to lean into the growth mind-set, you have to be willing to fall, make some mistakes, and feel the feels.

So my invitation to you is to start small by leaning into some opportunity or experience that you aren't certain you'll be any good at. I know, it's SO much easier said than done . . . but I've seen it done time and again.

I once worked with a client, let's call her Elaine (I have to be honest; it's getting really hard to come up with all of these fake names for clients). Elaine came to therapy to get help with her relationship with her husband, who had OCD—she didn't understand his OCD, felt burdened by it, and overall had very little patience for the way it inconvenienced her and the rest of the family. Now before we judge Elaine and assume she's just incredibly insensitive, you should know that it can be really hard to live with somebody who has OCD . . . not because they aren't lovable, but because their anxiety takes up so much time, energy, and space in the home. Elaine grew up in a family that, as she put it, "didn't do emotion." She had a hard time seeing it at first, but what she came to realize was that as much as she wanted to be empathetic toward her husband's experience, she couldn't because she was stuck in the fixed belief that men should be in control of their emotions, and she shouldn't have to support him, but instead he should support her. Deep breaths, because believe me, it was hard for me to not be judgy with this one too. The truth is, she was raised with parents who had a VERY fixed mind-set and did not make any room or space for emotion—she learned it wasn't safe to feel her feelings, so how could she respect her husband for feeling his? Elaine and I worked on things like talking about emotion and feeling and moved up the challenge ladder (so to speak), getting practice at validating her husband's difficult experience with his mental health as well as her own! In order for Elaine to make this shift and change, she needed to lean into vulnerability, the idea that she might not be good at this whole emotion thing . . . and if she could adopt a growth mind-set when it came to this, she could also adopt it in the other realms of her life.

LET'S WORK TOWARD CHANGE . . .

So, where do we start when it comes to cultivating a growth mind-set for ourselves and helping our children do the same? We start first by knowing that it's going to be hard to take risks, to lean into the possibility of the F-word (failure), so we'll need to be patient and graceful with ourselves. Then we pick some area of our life that we feel we could really benefit from cultivating a healthier mind-set around: maybe it's in your parenting style and how you encourage your children to take chances, maybe it's in the realm of career or creativity . . . wherever you recognize you often get stuck . . . go there. Once you figure out what that stuck point is for you, see if you can create some space around it by even just imagining doing something differently. If you've always wanted to start a blog but are worried you don't have enough to say, or that people would judge you, start with keeping a journal. Remember, it doesn't matter where you start, just that you decide to start. It will be worth it . . . I promise, both for you and for your children.

Who in your life do you admire for exhibiting a growth mind-set—somebody who has made mistakes but continues to keep moving forward or trying again?

When in your own life could you have benefited from adopting a stronger growth mind-set?

How willing are you to make mistakes or "fail" in the service of your values?

Pick one thing you're committed to trying/doing that is risky and uncertain, but you believe will help you grow. Take up painting, public speaking, or start a blog?

Chapter 10

YOU'RE INVITED TO CONSIDER THE SOURCE

"I carry a small sheet of paper in my wallet that has written on it the names of people whose opinions of me matter. To be on that list, you have to love me for my strengths and struggles."
—BRENÉ BROWN

Notice how I treaded lightly on the title of this chapter? I didn't do that because it's not an important invitation to accept, it may just be the most important yet, BUT our innate need for the approval of other people, to be seen and validated, is not something we can just do away with. Let me tell you a story about Oprah Winfrey—one of my sheroes. Oprah, who has interviewed pretty much every person under the sun (including criminals, thought leaders, movie stars, and presidents), says that the first question that EVERYONE asks when the camera is shut off or they step off the stage is some version of "How did I do?!" Oprah speaks of this phenomenon often, and notes that even some of the best speakers, including President Obama, have a need to know if they did OK. Crazy, right? But actually, Oprah (and I) think it makes total sense . . . because we humans are social creatures and we have a primal need, a longing, really, to be seen, heard, and validated. On the finale of her TV show, Oprah said: "I've talked to nearly 30,000 people on this show, and all 30,000 had one thing in common: they all wanted validation. If I could reach through this television and sit on your sofa or sit on a stool in your kitchen right now, I would tell you that every single person you will ever meet shares that common desire. They want to know: 'Do you see me? Do you hear me? Does what I say mean anything to you?'"

Since the need to be seen, validated, and approved of is a universal truth for all of us, I am not going to try to convince you (and you should be wary of anyone who does) that you need to shed your "give a shit." That's just not real . . . we care what people think of us, and we care a lot. And, regardless of what the cute Pinterest quote cards say, we will set ourselves up for failure if we think that we're going to wake up one day and suddenly not care what people think of us . . . unless it turns out we are sociopathic or narcissistic, and then we have more serious issues at hand. I think I'm in good company when I say that some of the popular culture messaging spread by influencers, and people without an education in psychology, telling us to just "not give AF" about other people's opinions is misguided and harmful.

WE SHOULD pay attention to how we make the people who have our best interests at heart feel and how they think about us. Reflecting on their experience of us and our actions gives us the important opportunity to make sure our intent lines up with our impact, and to apologize or correct course when we've caused emotional harm.

The truth is so much more complicated than if we proclaim we don't care what other people think anymore, we'll be total "bosses" and go on to #liveourbestlife. We are built to care, but we can care SO MUCH that it becomes unhealthy and problematic. When we let the opinions or judgments of those who don't have our best interest at heart, or who don't understand our experience, paralyze us or choose our path forward, we suffer for it. Caring too much about other people's opinions can cause us to struggle to make moves in our parenting, careers, and relationships EVEN when we know, on the gut level, what's best for us and our loved ones.

So I'm going to throw another "both and" your way. When it comes to how we hold other people's opinions or judgments about the way we are living our life, I think we need to make more space to turn inward and consider how our actions line up with our own core values AND make space for other people's feedback when (and only when) those people have our best interests at heart. We will talk more about how to determine what mirrors to turn toward, and what mirrors to turn away from (accurate mirrors versus fun-house mirrors), but first let's chat about WHY we are so attached to what other people think about us and our choices!

Since we humans are hardwired for survival, we have a need to be accepted and valued in order to stay "relevant" to our tribe (our family, communities, etc.). And, at the most primal level, we fear that if we aren't accepted, or valued, we will get kicked out of the very group that we depend on for survival and end up having to fend for ourselves. Thanks to time and progress, in today's world we no longer have to depend on our immediate family or community for actual survival (we have access to more options and resources), but a big portion of our emotional survival and sense of self-worth lies in their hands.

I could probably write an entire chapter (or book) on why women, in particular, tend to care a great deal about other people's approval, but I believe it stems from the cultural and societal notion that in order to be a "good girl," you need to be well-liked, palatable, and appeasing. Yes, it's total bullshit . . . but the notion that "good girls don't ruffle feathers" runs deep. Generations of women have tried to change that notion, but there's still so much more work to do . . . and it has to continue with us. The relationships we hold, and choose to foster, with people-pleasing and self-doubt is critical to breaking the cycle because our children (sons and daughters) are watching our every move and will learn so much more from our actions than they ever will from anything else. All that is to say, I hope you'll hear that you're not alone, or somehow flawed, for caring what other people think of you—we're all a product of what we see, learn, and hear throughout time.

So instead of trying to "rise above" something we are hardwired to care about, let's instead accept it as a part of the human experience and then learn the skill of pausing and reflecting to determine whether the opinion, criticism, or judgment being thrown our way is legitimately something we should listen to and turn toward, or something we should give little weight to and turn away from. What if we didn't buy into unhelpful messages that make us feel like we're weak for caring, and instead learned to give our own intuition and the small circle of people who support us (our personal advisory board) MORE weight than we give to the opinions of others who barely know us, or don't accurately see us? Now, my friends, we're getting somewhere.

There was an awesome meme going around recently that said something along the lines of "I'm in therapy to deal with people who need therapy!" Funny meme, but in all seriousness, I don't think I've ever read anything more accurate when it comes to why most people land at the door of my office, or on the other side of the screen. People have issues of all kinds, we all do . . . and while those issues are ours to own, when we don't work on them, they bleed into all the different parts of our lives, including our closest relationships.

There are a lot of reasons people don't work on their stuff (including unresolved trauma, stigma around getting help, lack of education on mental and emotional health, limited resources, lack of support, or sheer stubbornness), but whether it's a stranger on the Internet, your mom, your sister-in-law, or your old best friend, they likely don't see themselves as "wrong" or as having bad intentions when it comes to their opinions of you; they are "just being real or honest." The thing for us to realize (and often the hardest truth) is it's not our job to help them recognize their emotional illiteracy or change them—it's only our job to figure out how to lower their noise and turn toward a more accurate reflection. I've had to remind myself, my loved ones, and my clients of this truth often throughout my life; other people's opinions about you have so much more to do with them (and their "stuff") than they have to do with you.

When it comes to our own relationship with how we hold other people's opinions about our lives and how we're living them, it helps to think about the concepts of *fun-house versus accurate mirrors and people-pleasing.*

I'll talk more about how to determine who your accurate mirrors in the "let's work toward change" section of the chapter—but it's helpful to think of our accurate mirrors as the people who reflect back our whole image, whereas our fun-house mirrors reflect back a fragmented and disproportionate image of who we are. You've been to a carnival or a fair with those funky mirrors, right? The ones that reflect back a curved and distorted version of ourselves? They might make us laugh or take a second glance, but we know that's not how we actually look. There are people in our lives who act like fun-house mirrors. When we don't yet know how to do the work of tuning into our own truth and turning toward the people who really see us and are authentically rooting for our success, the voices of those fun-house mirrors (aka judgy people) can get REALLY loud and derail us on our path forward.

When it comes to all this "mirror" stuff, we have some choices to make. I know, just like you, that fun-house mirrors can be both disorienting and convincing, especially during times when we are about to take a leap or are feeling especially insecure, so we have to be intentional about how we respond to them. Here's a hard truth: sometimes the people we love the most can act as fun-house mirrors . . . and that's really freaking painful. Because it's easy to care less about what other people think about us when they don't play a leading role in our life than it is when they're VIPs. But the truth remains that the issue they have with our new business, style of parenting, or choice of hotel likely has to do with some hang-up or limiting belief they carry that has NOTHING to do with you. Surely we are invited to believe the fun-house mirrors and allow their distorted view of ourselves and our abilities to make us feel like we're not enough and suffer for it. But we are also invited to turn toward ourselves and what we know to be true about who we REALLY are and what we're really capable of (when we turn down all the noise) and the people in our lives who see us in all of our wholeness.

When we are overly invested in people-pleasing and being well-liked by all, it's even harder to unsee the image reflected back from the fun-house mirrors. I often call myself a "people-pleaser in recovery," because it's true that I battle with the deeply ingrained desire to please everyone in my life. The concept of people-pleasing certainly isn't foreign to most women—we first learned it as little girls through messaging from our parents, society, other influential adults in our lives that tied being a "good girl" with being helpful and appeasing. Then we had babies and literally HAD to put the needs of our tiny humans before our own, and got really out of practice when it came to asking ourselves what it is we want, need, or desire.

It's not bad to please people (it can be very rewarding), but when we choose to please other people before considering our own needs, wants, and desires, the cost is high . . . we start to feel lost, disconnected without sense of self and purpose, and risk experiencing resentment and overwhelm. It's hard to break people-pleasing patterns, especially when we've been at it for so long, but if we choose to stay attached to pleasing others at all costs, we will be the ones to suffer . . . maybe not now, but eventually. At the end of the day, we are the ones who have to lay our head on that pillow and think about whether or not we are living a life that feels authentic and in line with our values . . . nobody else.

MY INVITATION IN . . .

The best way to describe my attachment to what other people think of me is: "It's both complicated and in the process of evolution." I suppose that's how it goes, for most of us at least, when it comes to personal growth . . . it's imperfect, ever-changing, and evolving.

Throughout the course of my life, I can say with total confidence that I have BOTH spent too much time believing what the fun-house mirrors reflected back AND pleasing other people out of fear of not being liked or valued. But it wasn't really until I became a mom that I recognized I had this unhealthy attachment to other people's opinions. Because I have always (for the most part) found it easy to go with the flow of life, I never really minded other people's opinions—until I had babies and felt fiercely protective and

The moment she
remembered it
wasn't her weight
to carry, she was
once again free.

determined to do what was right for them, and right for us as a family.

Surely I don't have to remind you of this, because I know you've been there too . . . but people suddenly have WAY too many opinions once you become a mom. Unsolicited advice is EVERYWHERE for a new mom, and it can be so confusing and unhelpful. How you should feed your babies, sleep your babies, care for your babies, raise your babies . . . the list goes on. What makes it worse is, everyone seems to think they have the answer and that their way is the right way. Also, total bullshit. I wish I could say it came easier to me to disregard other people's opinions, but it wasn't, because there was nothing I ever wanted to get more "right" than parenting. Pre-kids, going with my gut seemed so much easier . . . but as a new mom, the stakes felt so high, and while I had a strong sense of what was right for us (that gut feeling) I often allowed the distortions from the fun-house mirrors to confuse my own sense of knowing.

I kept most of this struggle to myself (as we women tend to do) because I didn't want anyone else to see me as "weak" or "incapable," but all that doubt, paired with ALL the hormones, was just so exhausting and so overwhelming that I started to feel like I was drowning. While it's mostly a blur now, the first two years of my girls' lives were filled with so many beautiful moments and memories but also too much doubting myself and attempts to please everyone else except myself. When it comes to parenting advice, guidance can be helpful if it's done with grace and thoughtfulness, but it can also be other people's way of trying to validate their own parenting choices, which is totally unhelpful and distracting. While I can't change it now, and it was all a part of my own growth process, I wish I had tuned more into our actual lived experience than I did to other people's input on how I should "mom."

It wasn't really until I started to notice myself going through the motions of life and raising babies without a sense of presence or joy that I recognized something was "off" and desperately needed attention. It's not that I was NEVER present or enjoying time with my kids, and I recognize we put all kinds of unrealistic expectations around presence and savoring every moment, but more often than not it felt like something was missing. I likely had undiagnosed postpartum anxiety and depression, but another major culprit was my fear of other people's disapproval or judgment around my parenting. In therapy, and through my own self-work, I started to recognize the fun-house mirrors for what (and who) they were and choose to look inward for the truth. Once I started the very imperfect process of reclaiming and living into the kind of parenting that felt intuitive to me, I could then better recognize who my accurate mirrors were. I started spending less time Googling and listening to the judgy people and spent more time engaging in self-care and hanging out with people who were also choosing to live into their own truth. It felt SO good and SO freeing to be the parent I was instead of the parent I thought I should be. And by the way, there is nothing to humble you and demand you throw perfection out the window like having a third child and being outnumbered!

When it comes to motherhood and parenting in general, I have gotten pretty damn good at turning away from the fun-house mirrors, but when it comes to my career I still sometimes struggle. Why? Because I learned, in that fancy graduate school, that there is a "right" way to be a therapist. The "right" way (determined by a bunch of white men years and years ago) to be a therapist is to be a blank slate, ground your work only in evidence, and not personalize the work. While I started off my career doing things by the book, and I do believe that learning evidence-based practice is critical to developing a strong foundation as a therapist, it all started to feel so dehumanizing and robotic. I was worried though that if I listened to my gut and used both evidence-based practice AND my own unique ability to do healing work in a way that felt intuitive to me, I would be going against the tide, make too many waves, and be seen as not good enough. Bottom line, as women, it takes strength and conviction to do things differently—and those damn fun-house mirrors can make us feel like we're "ridiculous" or "off base" for doing things our own way.

But here's the thing, I recognized that I simply couldn't impact people the way I wanted to and continue to do the work of helping people heal and change, UNLESS I did it my way. It was uncomfortable as hell at first, and I got feedback from colleagues, family members, and friends (both positive and negative)—some who earned my respect and some who didn't—but ultimately I continued down the path because it felt true to me and my values. I started a podcast, a social media page, and took on writing projects all in the name of talking about mental health in a way that I hoped people would relate to, be able to digest, and then put into action. Because of the sometimes still uncomfortable choice to do things differently than how I saw others in my field doing it, I fell in love with the work and am constantly inspired by new ideas and possibilities when it comes to helping people live their best lives. Once we tap into our own authentic voice in the realm of parenting, our career, and our relationships, we can still fail, but we get the sense that we are "failing forward."

I don't get it perfect all the time, and I still find myself questioning and doubting my parenting and career choices, but the evolution happened when I gave myself permission to turn away from the stuff that didn't work for me, even when it went against other people's opinions, and turn toward what made me feel like I was living in line with my values, alive and seen. When I start to doubt myself or my choices, I am learning to listen, consider the source, and move forward in a way that honors my own voice and my own knowing.

YOUR INVITATION IN . . .

I've got to be honest, in the past I wasn't the person to make any big life decision (i.e., pick a school, a career, or even a relationship) without first seeking approval from my parents or closest friends. I wanted to move forward with the sense that I was doing the "right thing" (whatever that means), and let me tell you that all got so exhausting and disempowering. I still get a strange feeling when I make a bold choice without the approval of others—it feels a bit like when you're a kid and you sneak a cookie . . . but at the end of the day, I trust that I am capable of making choices that line up with my values—and I don't need to be told how to do that!

I am currently working with a client (let's call her Anne) who is stuck in the worry that she will be seen as a "bad friend" or "bad mom" if she doesn't do things a certain way. A little background on Anne: a few years before she started seeing me, Anne, who is also a therapist, decided to leave her church behind because she felt that there wasn't enough openness and empathy toward people who lived outside of the lines of what that religion deemed to be the "right" way to live. She didn't want to raise her children to believe it was "wrong" to be anything other than who they were. In leaving the church, Anne recognized how attached she had been for so long to doing things to "please" her church community even when it went against her own personal morals and values. While it was hard, she felt empowered and proud of her decision to live a life more in line with her values.

During the pandemic, Anne struggled with the isolation from her group of mom friends, whom she relied on for social interaction and as an outlet from the trenches of parenting . . . because we ALL need that! Anyway, because Anne chose to err on the cautious side, she often said "no" to social outings and worried that her friends would think she was "weird" or didn't care enough about them to see them. She also worried that people would judge her parenting and think that she wasn't offering her children enough social interaction. There was no evidence of her friends holding negative opinions (or opinions at all) about her choice to stay home, but the idea that they might hold those judgments was hard for Anne to sit with.

In working together, we recognized that Anne had some work to do when it came to her attachment to what other people thought of the choices that she made, choices that very much lined up with her values, which in the case of the pandemic was to keep her family safe even though she desperately missed socializing. After the wound of having lost her church community, she was afraid of losing her mom tribe.

I held up a mirror for Anne, just like so many have done for me, and reminded her that she is the powerful woman who decided to go against the tide and leave a social construct that was no longer serving her or her family. She was once that woman, and she still is . . . she just needed to remember to turn toward her truth, her accurate mirrors, and turn away from the belief that she needed to make other people comfortable rather than herself.

When it comes to the role we are going to allow other people's opinions (actual or perceived) to play in our life, we get to control the narrative. We can't just not care about what other people think, but we can (and should) make the informed decision as to whether their opinion holds value or just shade. We can't allow the voices of the critics to get so loud that we can't hear our own truth.

So how do we do this?

STEP 1: TURN INWARD FIRST. What do you think and feel about the choice/choices you are considering making in your life? What are the pros and cons of making that choice? How does making that choice (or not making that choice) line up with your core values? Practice self-reflection so that you can hear what it is you want or need first, and more clearly, before asking for outside input.

STEP 2: IDENTIFY YOUR ACCURATE MIRRORS AND SET A PERSONAL "ADVISORY BOARD." It's easy to identify the fun-house mirrors . . . they are the ones that we often leave an interaction with feeling like the life was somehow sucked out of us, and now it's a little harder to breathe. Fun-house mirrors make us doubt, question, and worry . . . sometimes they even gaslight us (make us question our own reality). Accurate mirrors see us, in all of our imperfection, beauty, and humanness. When we're engaging with our accurate mirrors, we feel seen, heard, validated, loved, and valued. After interacting with our accurate mirrors, we feel lighter, fuller, and more whole. Once we've figured out who the accurate mirrors are in our life, we should consider those people part of our personal "advisory board." It sounds a bit ridiculous, and we certainly don't need to put them on the payroll or anything like that, but we should consider this small circle of people the ones we can go to get support, constructive feedback, honesty, and love.

STEP 3: CONSIDER THE SOURCE . . . WHO IS WEIGHING IN? If it's a fun-house mirror throwing an opinion or judgment (shade) your way, you have full permission to consider the source and turn away. OK, I know it's not always so easy, especially if it's a family member, but you've got to make the choice to take care of your heart. If one of your accurate mirrors (your own voice or that of a loved one) is sharing an opinion and giving input, it should feel constructive and helpful. There is value in taking to heart other people's opinions so long as they have earned the right to share it with you, and so long as they have your best interests at heart. It is possible that somebody on your "advisory board" will disagree with a choice you have made, and that's OK . . . because when you are able to do the work of turning inward first, you can both take in their perspective and still decide that you want to move forward in a way that feels in line with your values. In my life, my mom (who is definitely on my personal advisory board) hasn't always agreed with my choices, and she isn't shy about offering her opinions. Sometimes I ask for her feedback, and it's truly helpful. OTHER TIMES (and I can hear her laughing at this) it's totally unsolicited and it's not helpful. The same goes for the other people on my advisory board, including my husband, a few of my best friends, and colleagues. I've learned that I can value their opinion and STILL choose to go forward in the direction that feels most true to my values, even if it means doing things differently than they would.

STEP 4: SAY YES TO YOURSELF BEFORE YOU SAY YES TO OTHERS. Do you ever know what you want or intend to do or how you feel, but still ask for other people's input and then change course based on that input? I hear you, because I do that too. That's really about wanting to get reassurance and make sure that our choice is going to be deemed "good" and won't upset anyone. Truth bomb: when we change course because we want to please everyone (something we can never do), we abandon ourselves. When we abandon ourselves, we get out of touch with who we really are and end up heading in directions that aren't right for us. When we practice turning inward before turning outward, by evaluating how we feel and what we think, we are honoring the knowledge that we can trust our gut, and that we are often our own best life expert.

Like every other process of growth and change, learning to not let our fear around how we might be perceived by other people control our narrative is a practice that we are invited to come back to over and over. When it comes to healing our relationship with other people's opinions and judgments, we are invited to first turn inward, reflect on our own core values, and then turn toward our accurate mirrors (personal advisory boards) for support and guidance. Hear this, you have FULL permission to turn your eyes and ears away from the fun-house mirror because we weren't given the gift of this life just to spend it pleasing everyone else. If you're anything like me, you'll definitely fall for the fun-house mirror tricks from time to time . . . and that's OK. Part of stepping into our power (and being the badass healthy adults we are) is learning how to course correct when we are off track. You are invited (always) to course correct.

What will your life look like if you continue to value the approval of other people before your own values, hopes, and dreams?

Let's flip the script: what would your life look like if you lead with your values (made choices only if they were in line with your values)? What would change? Who would stay around? What doors might close, and what doors might open?

If you could wave the magic wand and get rid of your fear around whether or not the people in your life will approve of your new business, new leap, life choice (the list could go on), would you move forward with your dream? Why?

What's one practical step you can start taking RIGHT AWAY (like today or tomorrow) to start practicing the skill of turning inward before turning outward and letting go of other people's judgments?

Chapter 11

YOU'RE
INVITED
TO SET
BOUNDARIES

"No is a complete sentence."
—ANNE LAMOTT

Boundaries . . . they're all the buzz these days, am I right? In the last chapter we talked about how damaging it can be to live our life for the approval of others, and the truth is, when we live for the approval of others we aren't able to honor the very important boundaries to protect ourselves, the relationships, and the "work" that is most precious and meaningful to us. If we aren't protecting ourselves, we sure as hell can't protect others—yet we (and me too) continue to work till we've got nothing left, put everyone else before ourselves, and take on the world.

Sometimes I wonder whether my grandma, who passed away about six years ago, would even understand what I was talking about if I were to tell her something along the lines of "I'm just trying to set better boundaries for myself." I am fairly certain she would have something awesomely offensive to say (she had the best and most offensive sayings like, "No man is going to buy the whole damn cow when he's getting the milk for free!"), but that's because, historically, women didn't have the right to much of anything at all (I mean we didn't even get to vote until 100 years ago) let alone the right to think about what boundaries would best serve themselves and their relationships. This isn't to say that there weren't women who took it upon themselves to blaze the boundary trails before us (women like Rosa Parks come to mind), but I'm pretty sure #boundaryconversations weren't getting the priority they are now! We are in a momentous time in history, when not only do we have the opportunity to change the narrative around our own roles as women in society but we have the opportunity to change it for our daughters, and just as importantly, our sons too.

I'm going to be crystal clear here, and while this goes against the social and cultural message that we've received for decades as women, I hope you'll give me some loud claps when you read this: setting boundaries doesn't make you a bitch, it makes you the boss . . . and you should be the boss of your own body, your time, the relationships you choose to hold, and the way you move through your life. Listen, as you'll hear in my own personal story around boundaries, I am far from an expert on the damn things, but I am learning that the more I set them and hold them, the more joy and peace I feel in my own life.

My hope is that this invitation will dive into the challenges with and importance of setting boundaries just enough for you to consider your relationship with setting and holding "the line" (so to speak) with yourself and your people (family, friends, coworkers, and Jody down the street). In fact, Jody down the street just might be the perfect person to start practice boundary setting on . . . no, Jody, I don't have to listen to you tell me how to handle my son's tantruming and "defiance" that is very much due to him being a typical three-year-old!

But before we dive in too deep with this whole boundaries topic, let's cover the basics and have a little review around what boundaries actually are, the primary types of boundaries, why it will benefit us to do the hard (and often awkward work) of setting the damn things in the first place!

WHAT ARE BOUNDARIES?

I am not Webster's dictionary, but here's my (imperfect) definition of boundaries: boundaries are limits or guidelines that we set for ourselves and others that allow us to love and be loved well. Boundaries are the ultimate form of care . . . care for self, care for others, and care for the world around us. The need for setting and holding boundaries is universal, whether you are a CEO, stay-at-home mom, mompreneur, teacher, bartender, or barista, you NEED boundaries. Why? Without boundaries, we simply can't preserve a healthy and wholehearted (yes, I'm going to use Brené's word again) relationship with ourselves or others. Speaking of Brené, whom you've probably noticed I'm a big fan of, she said something so very relatable and true about being courageous enough to have boundaries: "Daring to set boundaries is about having the courage to love ourselves, even when we risk disappointing others. We can't base our own worthiness on others' approval (and this is coming from someone who spent years trying to please everyone!). Only when we believe, deep down, that we *are* enough can we say 'Enough!'"

I think of self-boundaries as depositing money into your own bank of wellness. Self-care is one of the big buzzy words these days, but what does it actually mean? Self-care is respecting yourself enough to make the time to engage in the world in ways that feed your soul. As you'll hear in my story, and as you may recognize in your own story, we can't care well for ourselves when we don't have boundaries . . . it's just not possible. Here's what's true for me (and probably you too): when I decide (for the fourth day in the row) to skip my time for movement, or take a few minutes to hear my own thoughts, and say "yes" to time for everyone else except for myself, I am going to feel like crap and exhibit poor behavior (I've learned that adult tantruming is a thing). We need to schedule and protect time for ourselves to be human beings separate from our obligations to nurture, work, or perform. Speaking of self-care, it's not a one-size-fits-all concept . . . what fills up my cup (so to speak), or keeps me from being a mom monster, might be different for me than it is for you. For me, it's all about movement, meditation, and time to engage in creativity. Maybe for you it's a chat with your BFF on the phone, a pedicure, and a trip to Target just for fun. Whatever the heck it is that allows you to feel like a human being beyond a human doing, you have the right, and truthfully, the responsibility to make time and space for it. Yes, it's hard to carve out the time, there is no doubt that we have busy, full, and overloaded schedules but if we don't care for ourselves . . . let's be honest, it all falls apart.

Relational boundaries are about spending time and energy making guidelines that allow you to have healthy and lasting relationships. I'm not sure who said the words "clear is kind" or where I first heard them . . . but they resonated deeply. One of the things I've noticed throughout my years of working with women is that we seem to struggle the most with boundary setting and holding (because that's just as important as setting them in the first place) when it comes to our closest relationships.

Yes, if we are big old people pleasers (like I once was) we struggle to set boundaries across the board, but where it seems to hit us the hardest, or cause the biggest problems, is in our most valued relationships. I know it seems ironic, right? I think it's because we feel there is the most at stake with the people we are closest to (makes sense), so we're especially afraid of letting them down. If we grew up in a family where boundaries weren't held or respected (or even a "thing") the work of setting boundaries in our relationships as adults can feel especially hard.

Truthfully, though, if we don't set boundaries in our closest relationships, we will end up feeling resentful and tapped out, and the distance between us and them will grow bigger. Here's an example of setting a clear, kind, and respectful boundary in a relationship with somebody you care about: "I love it when you call, but it's best if we set a weekly time to talk because I want to be able to give you my full attention, however, I can't when I'm home with kids."

Holding boundaries is the place we often get stuck. So, I'm going to hit you with a truth bomb: boundaries are only seen as selfish to those who benefit from you having poor boundaries. People may have all kinds of reactions to your boundary setting, ranging from passive-aggressive comments to resistance and flat-out anger. It's not necessarily that boundary haters are "bad" people (I mean, they could be the worst), but it's likely that it's their own beliefs/fear that has them hating.

Maybe they're afraid that your setting boundaries (with yourself or them) will leave them getting less of you, or they'll lose out on something they were gaining from their relationship with you, like reassurance or their favorite pity party cohost. Or maybe they're just rocked by the fact that you're doing something that you haven't done before—you're changing the dynamic, and that can feel really uncomfortable to people who like the status quo. Lastly, maybe they just have really poor emotional literacy, engage in very little self-reflection, and think this whole personal growth thing is a total crock of shit/for hippies or self-entitled women who have too much time on their hands.

By the way, the belief that the work of self-reflection and personal growth is selfish and entitled IS what often keeps women like you and me from engaging in the work—and that belief is rehearsed (mostly) by people who are afraid of what it would mean for them to take a deeper look at their own lives, and the idea of you looking at yours threatens their own sense of security. Regardless of what their reasoning is for hating on your choice to set boundaries—the truth is, like I've said before, it's not about you . . . it's about THEM and their fears, reservations, and stuckness.

MY INVITATION IN . . .

How many times have you said "yes" to something that you really wanted to say "no" to? How many times have you forgotten about or stuffed down your own needs, or quieted the inner voice that was saying "for the love of GOD, don't do this again . . ." in order to please or make somebody else more comfortable? For me, the answer is (sadly) countless times. Even as I'm sitting here in this moment, about to start writing about boundaries, I am thinking about all the boundaries around my own self-care I have crossed this week. I am tired, sore, irritable, and stiff because I took on that extra client I swore I wasn't going to take, said "yes" to another podcast interview (that I don't get paid for), AND my daughter broke her arm . . . so there went that time for daily movement that I so heavily rely on.

So why did I say "yes" to the podcast and the extra client instead of my own sanity? Shitty boundaries. I think it was habit, really—I tend to have some periods of time where I do better with boundaries than others. I have a long history of saying "yes" to things out of fear of disappointing others or worry that if I don't take an opportunity in that very moment, it will never come again (scarcity mind-set). I see SO many people (including myself sometimes) blur the lines of their boundaries because they are afraid they will somehow lose out if they don't jump in with both feet. While that sometimes might be true, I think it's mostly the case that when we take care of ourselves and our primary relationships first, the opportunity to rise will come tenfold.

But going back to the whole broken-arm situation that happened this week—I wanted to be there with my daughter every second she was in pain to comfort her and love her, and I did my best to do just that—but since I had been "burning the candle at both ends" I was feeling tapped out with so little left to give. Yes, as moms we always rise to the challenge, but I am realizing that when I give so much to everyone and everything else, I have less to give to my most important people. OK, OK . . . it may not seem like it from the story I just shared, I've put a lot of work into my relationship with boundaries . . . and still it ebbs and flows and is very much in evolution. It's maybe not a pretty truth, but it's an honest one.

When it comes to pleasing friends and family (especially the ones I'm closest to) I have a hard time drawing a line in the sand, and my "flexibility," a quality that serves me well in a lot of ways, doesn't always serve me well when it comes to boundaries. I often feel caught in the crossfire of what I think other people want for me and forget what the hell it actually is that I want for me. Just the other day I said "yes" to going out to dinner with a group of friends and all nine of our (collective) kids and then remembered that both my husband and I felt really uncomfortable the last time we went because the location was close to a busy road, which is terrifying when you have a curious three-year-old, and there were drunk old men asking my little girls if they wanted to dance. When I told my husband that I accepted the invitation to go to dinner at a place we swore we wouldn't go to again, he told me that either he would call and politely decline or I could do it because we needed to stand firm in what was right for our family, regardless of how overly cautions or helicopter parentish our friends thought we were being. He held a mirror up for me, as the people we are the closest to often do (and should), and reminded me to hold the boundary that we set up thoughtfully and intentionally . . . even if it pissed people off.

Before you put this book down and think that I'm a total fraud for writing about a topic I am clearly no "expert" on—remember that I help people learn to set boundaries with themselves and others for a living . . . and I'm pretty good at it. Yes, yes, I know . . . we therapists are "supposed" to have our shit together, but as you know from my stories, that's just not true; we are practicing humans, just like everyone else.

So here's what I've recognized: I am a person (due to genetics, family of origin, culture, and a dose of perfectionism and anxiety) who has to constantly be aware of and evaluate my relationship with boundaries and whether I am honoring the very things I have put in place to protect myself and my most valued relationships. And just because I am passionate about my "work" in the world (it's up there high on my values list), it doesn't mean I have to make it all happen right here and right now—there is a sense of urgency I have around my creativity and my work that makes me forget to take care of myself, and THAT doesn't serve me.

Here's what I'm working on: I am working on giving myself way more permission to be direct and set boundaries with both myself and my loved ones. I'm working on my own commitment to getting movement in (mostly) every day, and spending some time working on projects that fuel me, saying "no" to social obligations that sound like . . . obligations, and shutting down the electronics when I walk in the door of my home. I am doing this because I recognize that I deserve to be in the driver's seat of my own life . . . even when that makes me, or others, uncomfortable!

YOUR INVITATION IN . . .

Boundary setting and boundary holding is something that comes easier to some than it does to others—there is no doubt that there is a wide spectrum when it comes to where we fall on our willingness to draw lines around both self and relational boundaries.

In my clinical work I find that most people I see struggle with boundaries to some degree, and that's no surprise because they're usually coming to me in the first place to get untangled from the messy emotions (like anxiety, worry, depression, apathy, resentment, overwhelm) that often stem from, or at the very least are made worse by, the poor boundaries they have in place for themselves and/or their relationships. Most women I meet with are just freaking EXHAUSTED from being in the throes of giving so much and receiving so little TLC from their relationship with their self (i.e., time to do the stuff that feels good) and the people in their lives. Raise your hand if you can relate . . . you can't see me but I'm raising mine too because, while I'm not there now, I've certainly been there before. It's not fun to feel like you belong to everyone else except yourself . . . it's maddening, confusing, and crazy-making all at the same time. The global pandemic made moms literally have to pull off miracles to manage all the moving parts (kids out of school, lack of childcare, working from home, I mean . . . I could go on), and so many women felt like they just didn't have anything more to give and experienced burnout at levels never seen before. While it felt incredibly hard for moms to have to pull off all the things we did during the pandemic, it also felt a bit like FINALLY being seen for all the shit we do on the daily. Suddenly there were news articles and segments on the *Today* show about "mom burnout" as if it were something new (excuse me while I roll my eyes).

The pandemic amplified the stress that is put on moms, but over the years, I've worked with many women who fit the profile of overextended, overwhelmed, highly perfectionistic, and in need of better boundaries. Take my client, let's call her Molly, for example. Molly's presenting issue (therapy term for why the hell someone decided to spend the money to come and see me in the first place) was feelings of depression and numbness. Like many of us, Molly found herself just sort of going through the motions of life, with very little feeling (good or bad) associated with the activities she used to enjoy, like socializing with her girlfriends or sneaking away for a date night with her husband. She noted that she did all those things (the dates, the coffee, the kids' pickup and drop-off, the smiles and waves, the work meetings), but she felt absolutely nothing while she was doing it, other than exhaustion.

I have to say, it seems that one of the scariest and most unrecognized kinds of depression is the kind that doesn't leave you locked up in your bedroom or crying at the drop of a hat, but instead the kind that has you feeling nothing at all. Why is it scary? Because feeling "nothing" or being "numb" is hard to see, and it's most often not seen or noticed either by ourselves or others as a typical symptom of depression, it often goes unnoticed . . . and then the person is left to suffer in silence. Suffering in silence is the ultimate suffering. A psychologist by the name of Margaret Robinson refers to

Setting boundaries doesn't make you a bitch, it makes you the boss ...and you were born with the freedom to make choices about all of the things that are yours to own.

this struggle as "perfectly hidden depression," and wrote a highly impactful book on how depression is often missed and undiagnosed in both women and men who are Type A high achievers.

Luckily, Molly had the self-awareness and insight to recognize, on her own, that something wasn't "right" and that she needed help. When we took a deeper dive into what Molly's life looked like—i.e., what her days looked like and who her time mostly belonged to—what we found was that NONE of it seemed to be dedicated to things that deposited money into her wellness bank. She was overwhelmed with her job as an ER nurse, which led to her feeling burned out and resentful, yet she never asked for time off or a shift change. She took on the majority of the stuff that needed to be done at home as well as the child-rearing, and she didn't ask for help from her husband because she didn't want to "complain." After she struggled so hard to have those babies in the first place, shouldn't she just be grateful?! Molly started to cry, the first time I noticed her seemingly feeling emotion, when I said, "Yes, you can be grateful AND overwhelmed AND in need of more help . . . just because you struggled to have them doesn't mean you have to live in gratitude every breathing moment . . . that's just not real life."

From there, the work with Molly was all about helping her define what really mattered to her, who the heck she was now at forty-five, and what kind of boundaries she needed to draw around her time and her relationships to allow her to experience living again.

LET'S WORK TOWARD CHANGE . . .

I know you know this by now if you have stuck with me this long, but the kind of work I did for myself and the kind of work I did with Molly around creating, firming up, and holding boundaries doesn't happen overnight. It can take a really f****** long time to get this shit right. But the thing that I hope you'll most glean from this chapter is that setting and keeping boundaries is the most loving, caring, kind, and fulfilling thing we can do for ourselves, our loved ones, and the work we do in the world, however big or small. You are worth the time it takes to find out what boundaries need to be reinforced for you to live most fully and in line with your values.

What is your relationship like with self-boundaries?

What boundaries do you consider to be most important in your relationships?

What (if anything) did you learn in your family of origin about boundary setting . . . and how might that affect how you perceive and utilize boundaries now?

If you lack healthy boundaries, or are recognizing the need to improve your boundaries, who do you think suffers the most from them . . . you, your loved ones, both?

What is one thing, person, place, event, task you can say "no" to today or tomorrow that might make you feel both uncomfortable AND relieved?

What do you imagine will change in your life when you continue to grow and evolve around boundary setting?

The Practice

Chapter 12

YOU'RE INVITED TO KEEP MOVING TOWARD YOUR MORE

"There is always light.
Only if we are brave enough to see it.
There is always light.
Only if we are brave enough to be it."
—AMANDA GORMAN

I wasn't sure which invitation to end this book with . . . but then I realized there really is no "end" when it comes to the invitation to grow and evolve. There is instead a continual invitation for us to lean into the opportunities to grow, to know ourselves and our relationships to the people and world around us better while keeping an open heart and open eyes. So as we are ending our book journey together, a journey that I hope goes far beyond these pages, I want to invite you to go (imperfectly) toward your version of more AND to be unapologetically you in every damn room you walk into! The truth is, I don't think we can successfully reach our version of "more" in life if we aren't willing to be our truest self. If you're thinking something along the lines of, "That sounds cool and all, but what does that look like?!" I'm here to tell you this: it looks like allowing yourself to take up the space you've earned in this world, and to have the courage to let your voice be heard even when that feels uncomfortable or unwelcome because (as you know by now) you're a grown-ass woman.

I know those words sound big, and maybe even a bit intimidating, but taking up space and using your voice doesn't mean you have to go starting a life-changing nonprofit (you can if you want) or tell your deepest and most vulnerable truths to everyone on the Internet . . . it simply means showing up in your authenticity. It could look like saying "no" to dinner at that relative's house who makes you feel uncomfortable with his creepy comments and rhetoric. It could look like saying "yes" to a painting night or an opportunity to speak. Showing up and taking up space in this world can look like a lot of different things . . . but here's the kicker: you're the only one who can do it and it will be hard at times.

Showing up as yourself—yes, in every room—will be especially hard when life throws extra shade and fun-house mirrors your way. But it's worth it. Because when we allow ourselves to show up as we are, and we stand tall and strong in who that person is, we make space for more. I don't know what your version of "more" is; it may be more present with your kids, it may be more open to what's beyond life as just "mom," or it may be more capacity to just enjoy your life as it is . . . all of that is worth the courage it takes to be authentic.

Remember your "big why"? I think the universal "big why" for most women when it comes to going for their version of more is both because we know, deep down inside and regardless of what the fun-house mirrors have told us, that it's our birthright to live our life in tune with our values AND it's our responsibility to show the generation after us (our babies) that they can and should do the same!

MY INVITATION TOWARD MORE . . .

I don't know what your "more" looks like—I only know what mine looks like now and how it's evolved over the years. I used to subscribe to the "once, then" mind-set. The "once, then" mind-set is something I totally just made up, right here in this moment, and it refers to the thought process of "ONCE (whatever the thing is) happens, THEN I will be (happy, satisfied, or successful)." But I've realized that every time I arrived at one of those places I was striving so hard to get to, it wasn't so much of a moment of arrival as it was a stairway leading me to the next step up. Take, for instance, my desire to have babies and become a mom. When I was in my twenties, I sort of (embarrassingly) believed that all I needed in this world was to find my life partner and become a mom . . . and that all this other "stuff" was sort of insignificant compared to that. I love being a mom—and being a mom has given me context and meaning beyond my imagination—but it's not like my wants and desires as a human stopped once I pushed those babies out. Instead, becoming a wife to an incredible human and a mother to my three (even more) incredible children only made me want to level up . . . to see what else life had to offer for me, and for us. If we integrate all the parts of ourselves, and allow ourselves to be a mother AND more, our capacity to love, give, and create only seems to grow.

So my version of "more" looks like not having all the answers and staying open to all the opportunities, even when they feel really freaking scary . . . like writing this book and sharing my truth and guidance (for what it's worth) with whoever will read it. My version of "more" looks like committing to being the most open, loving, and supportive mom, partner, daughter, sister, friend, therapist, and coach I can be. My version of "more" also looks like making MORE space for the things that feel deeply meaningful and lighthearted and fun (something I haven't been so great at in the past). "More" looks like quieting the voice inside that tells me I'm not good enough, smart enough,

When we give ourselves the gift of looking at and accepting all the parts of ourselves, we don't have to be anyone other than who we are . . . and that is true freedom.

pretty enough, ready enough, or qualified enough and taking imperfect action anyway.

My "more" isn't just one thing, or one goal that I've been striving to accomplish; instead, it's committing to a way of living my life that makes me feel most authentic and joyful, and gives me the space I need to be impactful in my relationships and creative work.

YOUR INVITATION IN . . .

The reason I chose the eleven invitations before this one is that they all seem necessary in order for us to be able to be our truest self and go toward our versions of "more." Once we accept the invitations to grow and evolve it's not like we're all done—we get to keep (imperfectly) committing to practicing the art of: walking through and understanding our story, feeling our actual feelings, determining our core values, welcoming uncertainty and anxiety as a part of life, challenging the stories we've come to believe about who we are and what we're capable of, practicing the gift of being present, increasing our psychological flexibility, cultivating a growth mind-set, working on our habit of pleasing others before ourselves, and holding on to the boundaries that protect our hearts and a healthy pathway forward.

Feels like a lot of work? I hear you. Accepting the invitations I've written about in this book takes courage and isn't for the faint of heart, but the payoff is immeasurable. The payoff is wellness—and wellness comes from staying in pursuit of a wholehearted life. Because when we are wholehearted and courageous enough to see beyond our stuck points . . . we get to see past the shit that keeps us from living our #bestlife and go toward our more. We won't always feel like a badass (you know that by now), because it's true that some parts of our story have and will continue to be painful, or challenging, or downright shame-inducing—but when we give ourselves the gift of staying open, curious, and accepting of all the parts of ourselves, we don't ever have to be anyone other than exactly who we are, or try to hurry the girl in the mirror to get to the person we're becoming . . . because we already are.

I don't want this book to end because it's been such a beautiful journey and a gift, really, to be able to spend this time with you—to get to share these invitations into growth and evolution while I'm also right alongside you doing the same work in my own life. On these pages live my story, so much of my heart, and absolute hope for you to be brave enough to step into your own growth, to embrace imperfection AND your way forward . . . your version of more.

For you, my biggest hope is that this work continues . . . that you keep remembering who you are, ask for what you deserve, stay curious and open when it comes to your own growth and evolution, and commit to pursuing the journey of living life in the way that feels most authentic, joyful, and meaningful to you. My hope is that if posed the same question asked by Mary Oliver at the beginning of this book, "What will you do with this one wild and precious life?" you'll answer it with some version of "I will choose to live it as the most wholehearted and free version of myself!"

I'll leave you with these words: *Growth and evolution are the acceptance of what was, and what is, and the openness to embracing the uncertainty, imperfection, and hope for what might be to come. We are doing the work of growth and evolution for us, and we are also doing it for them. . . .*

xoxo,

KAITLIN

Often when I read a book, I feel inspired and want to be able to put my new knowledge or growth into practice . . . but then life happens, and I forget. I don't want that for you!

I've said a lot in this book, and due to your own unique story and experience, some parts probably resonated more than others. There might be some parts that you still feel unclear around . . . or maybe there were invitations you weren't fully ready to step into. That's OK! I am going to invite you to come back to this book in a few months, but in the meantime, just let this learning (the stuff that stuck with you) live and breathe with you for a while. Right now, I suggest you put a reminder in your phone for three months from today to do some reflection work. Put an hour or so aside (I know that feels like a lot . . . but you're more than worth it), grab your notebook and favorite beverage, and have a little personal growth review date with yourself (look for those prompts on page 202).

But first, I'd like you to answer just this one question now, as you've wrapped up the final chapter:

What does your version of "more" look like now as a grown adult? What can you do, right away to start moving toward it? It can be simple, i.e, twenty minutes of movement a day (ish), finding a babysitter to come twice a week so you can work on a project or go for a hike.

Here are some questions I encourage you to ponder at the three-month mark. Go back to the journal prompts at the end of the chapters and ask yourself:

Do the things I wrote still feel true? Is there anything else I want to add or revise?

Is there an invitation that still feels unclear or that I am more ready to dive into than before? If so, reread that chapter!

What has changed within me since I've read this book?

What do I feel I am MORE capable of?

Am I taking imperfect action in the areas of my life that I value and hope to grow (i.e., parenting, career, spirituality)?

What does my version of "more" look like now?

Am I currently (and imperfectly) doing my best to live into my "more"? If not, what do I need? Do I need to ask for help from my partner or community? Do I need to create more time and space for myself again? Do I need to think about doing some one-on-one change or healing work with a therapist or a coach? What is it that I need to allow space for more?

Resources

Anxiety & Depression Association of America (*adaa.org*)

Books

Brown, Brené. *Daring Greatly: How the Courage to Be Vulnerable Transforms the Way We Live, Love, Parent, and Lead.* New York: Avery Publishing, 2012.

Brown, Brené. *The Gifts of Imperfection: Let Go of Who You Think You're Supposed to Be and Embrace Who You Are.* Center City, MN: Hazelden Publishing, 2010.

Doyle, Glennon. *Untamed.* New York: The Dial Press, 2020.

Gottlieb, Lori. *Maybe You Should Talk to Someone: A Therapist, Her Therapist, and Our Lives Revealed.* New York: Mariner Books, 2019.

Obama, Michelle. *Becoming.* New York: Crown, 2018.

Shannon, Jennifer. *Don't Feed the Monkey Mind: How to Stop the Cycle of Anxiety, Fear, and Worry.* Oakland, CA: New Harbinger Publications, 2017.

Tolle, Eckhart. The Power of Now: A Guide to Spiritual Enlightenment. Novato, CA: New World Library, 2004.

Podcasts

Super Soul Sunday, with Oprah Winfrey.

Trailercast, with Elyse Snipes.

Unlocking Us, with Brené Brown.

Acknowledgments

To the Collective Book Studio, thank you for taking a chance on an ordinary therapist/mom and believing that I had an important message to share. You made me feel so held throughout this process, making it so that I could stay in my "sweet spot," focus on the writing, and leave the rest to your wonderful team. Ruby, you are the world's most graceful, helpful, and supportive editor . . . I hit the jackpot with you!

To my kids, Mia, Alex, and Jack . . . you are the greatest gift, and you inspire me every day to be the biggest, boldest, and strongest version of myself. I don't always get it "right" when it comes to parenting, so thank you for giving me grace and teaching me what it means to love and be loved unconditionally. You are my wild, my greatest adventure, my whole heart, and my "why" behind everything I do.

Tony, my husband, thank you for believing in me every step of the way. Mostly, thank you for seeing me and loving me as I evolve, grow, and change—we could have never dreamt up this crazy little life our ours, but we sure know how to live it!

Mom and Dad, Bev and Dan, I am eternally thankful to you for giving me both roots and wings. You've guided me through so much throughout the years and raised me to believe that anything was possible so long as I was willing to put in the work and be brave enough to follow my heart.

And to my brothers, Ryan and Kevin, thank you for always having my back . . . no matter how busy life gets or how far we drift, I know you are just a phone call, and a few freeway exits, away.

Professionally, so many people have inspired me, but I want to thank a few in particular. Litsa Tanner and Jennifer Shannon (my mentors/first clinical supervisors), thank you for giving me a strong foundation to stand on, for sticking with me when I got pregnant two times in two years (as an intern), and for your continued support.

I also want to acknowledge Dr. Reid Wilson, Michael Thompson, Jennifer Shannon (again), and so many others I've been connected to via social media and podcasts—your contributions to the field of psychology and to my own understanding of what it means to be in the "helping" profession is immeasurable.

My own therapist and coach, Elyse Snipes—you have been the greatest gift and came into my life like both a wrecking ball (the kind I needed) and an angel. Thank you for helping me heal, find my voice, and learn to integrate all the parts of my story. You inspired me to lean into the most authentic parts of myself, even when I was scared, and (truly) it's from there that this book was born. I'll always remember you saying, "If you can't find your place at the table . . . create a new table." Well, here I am, creating my table.

And then, of course, there are my own personal "Shero's" made up both of my dearest girlfriends and people that have no idea who in the actual hell Kaitlin Soulé is! I have an affinity for thought leaders, and trailblazers, like Oprah, Brené Brown, Amanda Gorman, Glennon Doyle, and Mary Oliver—all of whom are incredibly brave and talented women who have blazed, and continue to blaze, the path forward toward wholehearted living.

To my girlfriends, who supported me throughout this journey and who continue to show up for me (even though I can't be on-time to save my life). I love and value you.

Also, I want to acknowledge myself. Okay, this part feels weird, but I'm going with it, because wouldn't it be weird if I wrote a whole book basically about honoring yourself and your worth, and then didn't honor my own? Thank you (to me) for saying "yes" to the book that was on my heart to write and sticking with it until the end even when it was emotionally and mentally exhausting to keep on keeping on.

Lastly, to all of you beautiful women who picked up this book—I hope you continue to choose to imperfectly grow and evolve. Never forget who the hell you are and what you're worth. And remember, you don't need permission . . . it's already yours to own.

About the Author

Kaitlin Soulé is a licensed marriage and family therapist, anxiety expert, and empowerment coach who resides in Northern California. She is a mom to three kids and identifies as a bit of a hot mess, a lover of the ocean, and somebody who is well versed in taking imperfect action. As a therapist, Kaitlin has an extensive background in providing cognitive behavioral therapy for children and families struggling with anxiety, OCD, and issues related to trauma. Through her social media platform, podcast, writing, and work in the field of mental health, Kaitlin empowers everyday women to take control of their life, and regardless of their past, steer toward their best and most authentic future. Kaitlin's larger mission is to be a part of dismantling the belief that therapy is only for the "broken" and to empower women to take control of their life's narrative by investing in their own mental/emotional growth and evolution so they can live their most meaningful and joyful lives.

Email: *kaitlin@wellnotesbykaitlin.com*
Instagram: *@kaitlin.soule*